JACOB THE RIPPER

THE CASE AGAINST JACOB LEVY

TRACY AND NEIL I'ANSON

MANGO
BOOKS

Published by

Mango Books
www.MangoBooks.co.uk
18 Soho Square
London W1D 3QL

JACOB
THE RIPPER

CONTENTS

INTRODUCTION

Jacob Levy came to our attention many years ago. Since that time we have set out to raise his profile as a suspect for the mantle of Jack the Ripper. Jacob was no itinerant visitor; he fit the basic profile and more, and most importantly: he was there.

Our continuing research has brought new evidence to light; sifting through hundreds, if not thousands, of pages of information from various research facilities we came across new undiscovered facts that strengthened our theory, and helped us piece together the life of Jacob Levy.

While we recognise that the 'meat' of any book putting forward a candidate for the dubious mantle of 'Jack the Ripper' is the evidence against the suspect, it is important to place this series of murders in their context of time and location.

The victims of the Whitechapel murderer have, over the years, been often vilified, purported to be lowly, unworthy members of society not deserving of compassion or sympathy. Some writers have even stated that they deserved their fate. In this book we hope to convey a more realistic view into their lives. Our aim is to show them as normal people who, like most of us, perhaps didn't always make the right decision, and as a result caused some of the problems that they faced in life. They were also women with families and friends, trying to live their lives as best as they could given the difficult circumstances they were faced with.

We take a look at what Victorian life was like, and how people lived at the time. We touch upon how the media used the killings to their advantage, selling more newspapers than ever before by feeding public hysteria and sending readers into a frenzy with each new murder.

Our book goes some way to explaining the movements of Jack the Ripper, the graffiti, the actions of the police, the 'Lipski' link, and ultimately what happened to the murderer.

We hope the accumulation of facts in this book makes you consider the validity of our claim. We have tried to keep it interesting and informative without being critical of anyone else's opinions and beliefs.

TRACY and NEIL I'ANSON
July 2020

NEIL I'ANSON was born under the sign of Aries in a little village in Yorkshire. He was just five when his father died and the family moved to north east England, where he now resides. Neil's desire when he was a teenager was to become an archaeologist but he couldn't spell it, so he became a butcher instead, working in the meat industry for five years before entering the retail management field. Neil has been married since he was 21 and has two children and two grandchildren. Since his retirement he has loved walking around the countryside with his dog. His interests are gardening, sport and anything to do with history, be it family or social (he's just plain nosy). His greatest love is his family.

TRACY I'ANSON was born in the late 1970s and admits she is the perfect example of a Gemini – never being able to stick to one project at a time. Her love of history and true crime begn at an early age, spending many nights with her father Neil discussing historical crimes, and her interest in genealogical research was stimulated by her own family tree which has now been traced back to the 14th century. She admits she is lucky to love the job she has, managing a pub that also includes giving tours round Camerons brewery, to which the pub is attached. In guiding visitors around the brewery explaining how it works as well as describing its history, Tracy gets to incorporate her two loves in life – history and beer.

1.

POVERTY
IN VICTORIAN LONDON

One of the reasons for Jack the Ripper's success/anonymity was the overcrowding and poverty of London's East End.

Victorian London was the jewel of the British Empire, a fount of industry, culture, abstinence and justice – or so we are led to believe. In reality, London was a cesspool, rotten to the core. By the Victorian period Whitechapel in the East End was notorious, a thieves' kitchen and a refuge of whores, earning itself a reputation with not just growing numbers of the destitute but also of 'clippers', pickpockets and footpads, who would attack and then disappear into the maze of passages and alleyways that abounded in the tightly-knit area.

The formation of Whitechapel's overcrowded, pestilential vice-ridden roots can be traced back as far as Henry VIII and the dissolution of the monasteries. During Henry's reign the population of London increased from 50,000 to 200,000. Henry sold off land belonging to the Roman Catholic church, and the changes in land ownership and subsequent usage were greeted with glee by the rich, along with Henry's courting of selective European immigrants to bring their industrial techniques and skill to his court. The already suffering poor, however, having lost their almshouses and nunneries, now faced upheaval and urbanisation.

John Stow (1525-1605) was a tailor who spent all his life in Aldgate. He is most well known today for his 1598 work *Survey of London,* a historical and topographical survey of the capital that became an invaluable source of information. Stow voiced his fears over the already overcrowded East End, which also being a health hazard to its inhabitants, was also becoming a potential health hazard to its more affluent neighbours. This led to the limiting of new property there. The result was futile, however, as the result was more people being squeezed into less space, making properties more crowded and even less sanitary than before.

This set the blueprint for Victorian London. Money and finance would be the lifeblood of the City, while Government and retailing would lie to the West of London. Manufacturing, processing and finishing, with all their attendant dangers, would be in the industrial quarter to the East.

Industrialisation had led to more people seeking a better life in towns and cities, with many new factories being built. In 1801 nine million people resided in London, yet unbelievably in 1901 forty-five million people lived in the same area. When you consider fifteen million transient people travelled to England, mainly London, before emigrating on to America and Australia, it is understandable that the already overflowing buildings couldn't cope. The desperate shortage of housing was exacerbated in the 1870s and '80s, when the Pogroms of Eastern Europe resulted in an influx of fleeing Jews into London, adding to the large Jewish population already residing in there. They settled alongside people who had moved from rural areas, as the potato famine in Ireland throughout the 1840s had led to countless Irish people moving to London, fleeing poverty and famine to find a better life.

As London grew, pressure on building space made any open land a target for the Jerry builder: old market gardens, former farmland and marshy meadows were all utilised by 'fag end' builders to erect slum dwellings, leased for twenty-one years from Crown or Parliament Officials. There was no desire to build dwellings of a longer lifespan, instead buildings were erected with no foundations, walls of just half a brick thick – basically tiles – unpaved yards, and streets without drains.

It was to deal with places such as this that a new Law was passed, the Metropolitan Management Act, which created the Metropolitan Board of Works; a body to coordinate the construction of London's infrastructure. Local parish councils would be responsible for public health, while the London Metropolitan Board of Works would set about draining London, driving new streets through the congested district, and later clearing slums. Along with the clearance schemes by the Railway Companies, these improvements often created more overcrowding.

Charles Cochrane, the chairman of the Poor Man's Guardian Society, wrote a vivid and descriptive account of the filth and putrid conditions in which residents of Field Lane were living in an in-depth and evocative article published on 20th November 1847:

> *Amongst other offensive matter which arrested our attention were dead cats, in a semi-putrescent state. We were, however, assured by the parties connected with this horrid establishment, that the filth and dead animals referred to, were thrown into the cellar from the street and were frequently being removed by the dustmen. As I proceeded to question them more closely on these points, I found their answers so unsatisfactory, that I doubt very much if the dustmen pay them many visits during the year.*

In particular, it's interesting to note what Cochrane has to say about the wash house. Elsewhere in London, when there was a new development of dwellings, a wash house would be created, usually in the cellar. Within a month of the Field Lane dwellings being opened and occupied, four of the poorer families resided, slept and lived their daily lives amongst the sinks and laundry of other residents.

Ongoing slum clearance in the 1860s is estimated to have displaced as many as 56,000 people, mostly poorer working classes, from their homes. It wasn't until the first slum clearance measure – the Artizans' and Labourers' Dwellings Improvement Act of 1875 – that London was able to strike at the heart of the city's overcrowded disease-ridden slums.

Work, when it could be had, was hard. Wages for a man was typically fifteen shillings a week. Women and children were paid much less; women earned only seven shillings and children three shillings a week.

Many boys were sacked on reaching adulthood due to the fact that employers had to increase their wages, and consequently many men had to be supported by their families.

Although there were advocates for reform, many spoke out against changes. The economist Nassau Senior argued that increased costs would ruin the economy, while some people argued that the extra leisure time and money would only be spent on crime and drunkenness. Even the Government believed it should not involve itself in the free working of the economy.

It was against this background of antipathy and despair that mothers and wives tried to build a better life for themselves and their families, but for the huge majority this wasn't easy. At work many women were beaten, which was known as strapping; at home some women were also beaten by their husbands, who saw it as their duty. Women were treated daily as chattels, with no rights or say over their own lives. They were seen as second-class citizens.

William Acton (1813-1875), a doctor specialising in sexually transmitted diseases, was interested in how and why these occurred and their impact on the community. He was the first person to publish a report on the state of prostitution in Victorian England, in his *Prostitution Considered In Its Moral, Social And Sanitary Aspects, In London And Other Large Cities* of 1857. It was considered an epic work. At a time when prostitution was viewed as the scourge of man, Acton's report came across as balanced and sensitive. He called for an end to classing women as 'outlaws', and rejected the popularly-held opinion that women had chosen prostitution because they held an innate sinfulness. Instead, Acton highlighted the social conditions that drove the women into the oldest profession, including hunger and distress. They were driven by poverty, worthlessness and despair to a gin-soaked existence in the doss houses and streets of East End London, debasing themselves through alcohol and sex for sale in a search for the most basic of life's necessities: sleep, warmth and food.

2.

VICTORIAN POLICING

When the Whitechapel murders took place in 1888, the police force we still know today had been in existence for almost 60 years. It had been introduced by the then Home Secretary Robert Peel, who devised the Metropolitan Police Act of 1829. Until then, from 1674 the law consisted of either a Constable, a Justice of the Peace or a Watchman. Parish Constables were required to apprehend anyone believed to be guilty of a crime and take them before a Justice of the Peace; however, they were not obligated to investigate or prosecute any crimes. Night Watchmen usually patrolled the streets throughout the night until dawn and were there to deter any criminal activity.

It was normal practice for a victim of a crime to identify and apprehend the offender, if they could, before finding a constable to arrest them. Witnesses to a crime were legally required to apprehend the felon, and bystanders were legally obliged to go to the aid of a constable if he needed assistance whilst in pursuit of a criminal or suspect.

Robert Peel's vision was to create a full-time, centralised, professional law enforcement agency that consisted of a clear hierarchical structure and chain of command, all under the control of the Home Secretary. This would not include the City of London, which would soon after create its own force, the London City Police, which operated within the historical square mile of the City. In 1839 it would change its name to the City of London Police.

The Metropolitan Police Act established the so-called New Police, which would be responsible for the whole of the Greater London area, replacing the locally-elected watchmen and parish constables. It consisted of seventeen divisions, each of which had four inspectors and 144 constables. The police headquarters were situated at Great Scotland Yard, and its aim was to emphasise preventative policing and surveillance, which required the officers patrolling a particular route at a set time in a shift pattern – a 'Beat'.

Robert Peel's new force, often nicknamed 'Peelers' or Bobbies', were given a uniform consisting of long blue coats and strengthened top hats that would protect them from a blow to the head. They also carried a pair of handcuffs, a wooden truncheon (which was the only weapon they were allowed to carry) and, originally, a rattle to call for help, although this was eventually replaced by a whistle.

Joseph and James Hudson, whose company had manufactured whistles which were the first used by football referees since an 1878 cup match between Nottingham Forest and Sheffield, put forward their 'police whistle'. This new whistle had been invented by Joseph Hudson and contained a pea, which resonated loudly enough that the noise could be heard for over a mile away. The Metropolitan Police were the first to use the whistle, but it was quickly adopted by the rest of Britain.

Although Peel's organisation was eventually a success, it wasn't immediately embraced by the public as people believed the New Police would be a threat to their civil liberties.

In 1877 the so-called Turf Fraud Scandal brought great public embarrassment to the force when three officers from within the Detective Department were found guilty of corruption. This resulted in a complete reorgnisation of the Department, with the new division renamed the Criminal Investigation Department (CID). Strangely, the head of the CID, Charles Howard Vincent, would be responsible only to the Home Office and not the Metropolitan Police Commissioner, but the officers underneath him were responsible to the Commissioner and not the Home Office.

It is easy for people today to look back on the case and question how and why the police didn't catch the Ripper. In Victorian times policing was still in its early days; the police work and investigation they did was, for the most part, commendable. These were the days before forensics such as fingerprinting and blood-group identification, let alone DNA. They were faced with obstacles such as poorly-lit streets, the warren-like dens of the East End and limited means of contacting one another, not to mention the many dozens of dead-end leads which needed to be investigated and eliminated.

That said, despite these obstacles the policemen of 1888 still walked the streets questioning people, knocking on doors and businesses. They also learned 'on the job' as the series of murders unfolded, assimilating facts to refine the ways in which they searched and questioned witnesses, to the methods they used to assess the crime scenes. In fact, Mary Kelly's bedroom was the scene of the first-ever crime scene photographs. The murders also saw the first attempt at a criminal profile, by Scotland Yard's Divisional Surgeon Dr Thomas Bond.

3

MARTHA TABRAM

Martha White was born on 10th May 1849 at Marshall Street, London Road in Southwark to Charles Samuel White, a warehouseman, and Elizabeth White née Dowsett. Martha was the youngest of five children, after Henry (b.1837), Esther (b.1839), Stephen (b.1841) and Mary Ann (b.1846).

In the 1851 census the family were recorded as still living at Marshall Street. As of yet we haven't managed to locate Martha and her family in the 1861 census. There could be numerous reasons for this – a transcription error, an enumerator error, the family gave their name to something else, or even just they didn't want to take part in the census.

Charles and Elizabeth separated in May 1865, and Charles began lodging at 31 Pitt Street, St George's Road. He was still there on 15th November, when he died suddenly aged 59. Three days later his inquest was held at The Gibraltar public house in St George's Road, conducted by William Payne, the Coroner for the City of London and Borough of Southwark. It was recorded that Charles died from natural causes.

On 25th December 1869, at the age of 20, Martha married Henry Samuel Tabram, 13 years her senior, at the Holy Trinity Church in Newington. Henry was recorded as a widower and Martha a spinster. They were both living at Pleasant Place, and his profession was simply noted as 'packer.' Henry's father was named as John Steward Tabram, deceased, and Martha's father was Charles Samuel White, also deceased.

Henry had been married previously to Matilda Ann Mayes and they had children of their own – Henry Thomas (b. 1860), Matilda (b.&d. 1864), Matilda Ann Hannah (b. 1865) and Amy (b.&d. 1868). Henry's first wife Matilda died in the second quarter of 1869, aged 31.

A newspaper article in the *Clerkenwell News* of 4th January 1869 reports of a violent assault against a Martha Tabram:

Clerkenwell Police Court, January 2nd.

Violent Assault – Henry Tabram of 60 George's Road, Holloway, was brought up in the custody of police constable Henry Robinson 88 N, one of the warrant officers of the court, charged with assaulting Martha Tabram, his daughter in law.

Mr Ricketts, solicitor prosecuted.

Both parties lived in the same house, and some words ensued between them about a saucepan. The defendant called the complainant a b------ cow and, without any provocation, he struck her across the head and thigh with the saucepan, and caught her by the hair of the head and dragged her round the room. The complainant has been deserted by the defendant's son, who is now living with another woman, and the defendant and his son are both bound over to keep the peace towards her. Had it not been for assistance coming to the complainant the defendant would have illused her worse than he did.

The defendant said he was sorry for what he had done, and if the magistrate would look over it this time he would take care not to offend any more.

Mr Barker ordered the defendant to pay £2 4s., or in default to be imprisoned and kept to hard labour in the House of Corrections for one calendar month.

The defendant was locked up in default.

Another article which appeared in a few newspapers from that year commonly accepted to be about 'our' Henry and Martha reported how Henry Tabram and his paramour threatened Martha in a drunken row.

MARTHA TABRAM

The report below from the *Islington Gazette* dated 12th October 1869 gives the fullest account of events:

A husband and his paramour threatening to murder the wife. – Henry Tabram, a costermonger, of Starkey's Yard Islington, and a woman named Peck, who cohabited with him were charged with using threatening and menacing language to Martha Tabram, by which she went into fear that they intended to do her grievous bodily harm.

Mr Ricketts, solicitor, appeared for the complainant and Mr John Wakeling, solicitor, for the defence.

The complainant stated that owing to the drunken and brutal behaviour of her husband, who had been charged with assaulting her, she and her family of six children were now living away from him, he agreeing to allow her 6s per week for their support, but she had received no money for a fortnight. A few days since her husband and the woman Peck, who lives with him, came to her residence, and seeing her at the window, called her most filthy and disgusting names. Her husband told her to come down, and he would hold her whilst his paramour pulled her ------ guts out. They both said they would do for her, and remarked that if they could not carry into execution their threat on that occasion they would whenever they met her out. Both the defendants were drunk and some of the bystanders took up the cudgels on behalf of the wife, and hooted and pushed the defendants away.

Mr Wakeling, for the defence, said that the court ought to take no judicial notice of bad language used when the defendants were drunk, and that it was mere idle threats that were used, whilst Mr Ricketts contended that the conduct of both parties was very bad, and deserving of severe punishment.

The magistrate remarked that the conduct of both defendants was disgraceful in the extreme. What they had done was improper, but still the threats were used when they were drunk, and as, he didn't think the complainant had anything to fear the complaint was dismissed – When the husband and the woman he cohabits with got outside they were set upon and narrowly escaped a severe handling.

From these newspaper articles it does appear at first glance to be 'our' Martha and Henry Tabram. However, further research shows that it was in fact a different family. It's likely that the Martha Tabram mentioned in the articles was in fact born Martha Mosely in Kingsland, Middlesex in 1836. This Martha married a Henry Thabram, and the children's baptism records them living at George Road. Finally, Henry's father is also named Henry. These facts corroborate with the information given in the first newspaper article.

In February 1871 Martha had given birth to her first child, Frederick. In the 1871 census they were noted as living at 20 Marshall Street. Living with them also was Henry Tabram, Henry's son from his first marriage. In December 1872 Martha gave birth to their second child, Charles Henry Tabram.

By 1875 Martha and Henry had separated again, apparently due to her excessive drinking. Henry stated he provided her twelve shillings a week, according to *The Times* of August 24th 1888.

Records showed that on 5th October 1876 Martha Tabram, now aged 25, discharged herself from the Newington Workhouse on Westmoreland Road in Southwark. Her last meal before being discharged was her breakfast. She was admitted back to the same workhouse on 31st May 1877. Her date of birth was recorded as 1849, and she gave her age as 28. Her religious persuasion was noted as Church of England, and the parish she was admitted from was St George's Parish. The observations column noted the handwritten letters 'dest'. This could signify either deserted or destitute, either of which could be used to describe Martha's circumstances. She was also noted as being married, and her calling was simply recorded as 'needle'.

On Thursday 28th June 1877 both of Martha's sons were admitted to St George's Workhouse in Mint Street, Southwark. At this time Frederick was 7-years-old and Charles aged 4. Their next meal after admission was to be supper. They were both noted as Church of England in the religious persuasion column, and had been admitted from Newington. In the observations column it was noted that they were from Hanwell schools. The following day, 29th June, both boys were discharged after breakfast along with their mother, who was discharged at her own request.

On Wednesday 1st May 1878 the boys were admitted to the Broad Street Workhouse in Holborn. Both were classed as 'child porters', and this time were recorded as being of Roman Catholic denomination. They were admitted by the Relieving Officer, and in the next column for both boys the remark 'PC 287E' is noted, presumably the collar number of the policeman who brought them in.

They were discharged from the workhouse on Wednesday 15th May 1878. Both boys had been given dinner before discharge, and the 'How discharged' column noted that the boys went 'To mother at prison.' As yet we've been unable to find out why Martha was in prison. According to a report from the *London Advertiser* of 25th August 1888 covering Martha's death, her sister-in-law Ann Morris told how Martha had been up against the magistrates three times for bothering her, and the last time she was sent to prison for breaking her windows. While we can't confirm it, it is possible this could be why she was in prison in 1878.

A few weeks later, on Saturday 1st June 1878, Charles was charged with begging and placed in the Westminster Union Workhouse. There was no age stated for him this time, but the entry did show that he was born in 1873 and was Church of England. He had been admitted from St James' Parish, and in the observations column is written 'Off Vine Street Station.' On his discharge on 14th June he was released to his mother.

The final entry that year for the family came on Friday 20th December, when it was recorded that Martha Tabram, aged 26, Frederick, aged 7, and Charles, aged 5, entered the Newington Workhouse on Westmoreland Road in Southwark. Martha's occupation was given as 'Slipper maker', and they were all admitted from St George's Parish. Martha was noted as 'married', and Frederick and Charles were recorded as 'deserted'.

The boys were discharged on Monday 13th January 1879, according to the observations column 'to St George's.' Martha was discharged on Friday 9th May 1879 at her own request, leaving after her dinner. For some reason she was recorded as being 29-years-old.

Sometime in 1879 Martha met Henry Turner, a carpenter, and they quickly became an item. Once her husband Henry Tabram found out she was living with Turner he reduced the amount he paid her each week to 2s 6d.

In the 1881 census, taken on 3rd April that year, Martha is listed as residing at 35 Thomas Street, Whitechapel, a known workhouse. She was recorded as being 30-years-old and a flower hawker. Frederick and Charles were also there, albeit with their ages listed incorrectly.

Two weeks later, on Sunday 17th April, Frederick and Charles were admitted to the Stepney Workhouse, Tower Hamlets, brought in by PC 32K. They were discharged on Monday 25th April at 10.30am, this time 'taken out' by PC 34K. Just three days later, on 28th April, the boys were admitted to the Fulham Road Workhouse, Westminster, classed as destitute. The following day they were discharged into their mother's care.

The final record we discovered is from St George's Workhouse, Mint Street in Southwark. On Friday October 15th 1886 Charles Tabram, now aged 13, was admitted into the workhouse from St George's before supper. He was brought in by PC 145M. The following day after dinner he was discharged into the custody of the same constable.

It is worth mentioning that the workhouse information given above comes from the actual workhouse records; it is accepted that the Fulham Road Workhouse noted in the register was actually situated in Palace Road, which is located in Chelsea not Westminster as documented. Likewise, the St George's workhouse was actually situated in St Saviour, not Mint Street as stated.

In April 1888 Martha and Henry Turner were lodging with Mary Bousfield at 4 Star Place in Whitechapel. They left without paying two weeks' rent, although according to the *East London Advertiser* of 25th August 1888 Martha did sneak back and return the key. By July 1888 Martha had left Henry and moved to 19 George Street, a common lodging house in Spitalfields. Later, at the time of the inquest into Martha's death, Henry was residing at the Working Men's Home, Commercial Street in Spitalfields.

Around 11.00pm on Monday 6th August – a Bank Holiday – Martha was seen in Whitechapel Road by her sister-in-law, Ann Morris. Ann was described at the time of the inquest as 'a very respectable woman', dressed quietly in black. She lived at 23 Fisher Street, Mile End and said she was a widow, the sister of Mr. Tabram, the husband of the deceased. Martha then met up and spent the evening with a friend, Mary Ann Connelly, known as 'Pearly Poll'.

A couple of hours later, between 1.40 and 2.00am, Joseph and Elizabeth Mahoney returned to their lodgings at 47 George Yard Buildings. Elizabeth left again shortly afterwards to a chandler's shop in nearby Thrawl Street for some supper, and returned home just five minutes later. She later testified that she neither saw or heard anything unusual.

PC Barrett was on duty around George Yard Buildings at 2.00am when he spoke to a Private in the Grenadier Guards who was standing at the entrance to George Yard. The Private informed the policeman that he was just waiting for his mate, who had "gone off with a girl".

At 3.00am Alfred Crow returned to his room at 35 George Yard Buildings. He did see a shape on the first floor landing but just assumed it was someone sleeping there, a frequent occurrence.

John Reeves, who lived at 37 George Yard Buildings, left for work at 4.45am. On the first floor landing he found the body of Martha Tabram lying in a pool of blood. Without touching the body he went to find a constable and returned with PC Barrett, who had been nearby continuing his beat.

PC Barrett immediately sent another constable for Dr Timothy Killeen of 68 Brick Lane, who took Martha's body to the mortuary shed in Old Montague Street for a post mortem.

The inquest was presided over by Mr George Collier, Deputy Coroner for the South Eastern Division of Middlesex, and took place at the Working Lad's Institute, Whitechapel Road.

Henry Tabram appeared and after giving his address of 6 River Terrace stated that he had last seen Martha about eighteen months previously in Whitechapel Road. He told the inquest that they had separated thirteen years previously because of her drinking habits. He also stated that she had got up a warrant against him, but didn't specify as to what it was for.

THE DISCOVERY OF "JACK THE RIPPER'S" FIRST MURDER.

Henry Turner, who had lived with Martha until a few weeks prior to her death, also testified. He told the inquest that he had lived with Martha as his common-law wife for about nine years before the recent split. He did admit that he had left her twice in the past due to her drinking, but they had got back together. He'd last seen her three days previously in Leadenhall Street, when he had given her one shilling and sixpence to buy some stock to hawk, a common way for people with no trade in Victorian times to make money, although normally it was barely enough to get by. Henry acknowledged at the inquest that Martha was a woman who, when she had money, would 'get drink with it'. While he told the inquest that he didn't believe Martha walked the street while she was with him, he did acknowledge at the inquest that sometimes she would have stopped out all night and that she told him it was due to fits and she had been taken to the police station.

Mary Bousfield, who lived at 4 Star Place and rented a room to Martha, said that she and Turner had left in mid-July without settling their debts, owing two weeks' rent. Mary said that Martha would prefer a glass of ale to a cup of tea, but despite that wasn't a woman who was always drunk. She was sure that Martha never brought any companions back to the lodging house, and she believed that she earned a living by hawking items such as matches, needles, pins and menthol cones. Martha had told Mary that she had been living with Henry Turner, who was very good and helped her support her two children, although Mary had never seen them.

Mrs Ann Morris, Martha's sister-in-law, told the inquest she had last seen Martha on the night of her death at about 11.00pm in Whitechapel Road. Martha had been about to enter The White Swan public house.

Another witness at the inquest was Mary Ann Connelly, known as 'Pearly Poll'. She was cautioned in the usual manner by Inspector Reid and sworn in, then stated that she was a single woman and had known Martha for about four to five months, although she had known her by the name of 'Emma'. Pearly Poll last saw her alive on the Bank Holiday night when she was with her for about 45 minutes. They were with two soldiers, one was a Corporal and the other one a Private, regiment unknown. They parted around 11.45pm, Pearly Poll taking the Corporal to Angel Alley and Martha going with the Private up George Yard. She stated that Tabram wasn't too drunk, but they had been drinking ale and rum.

PC Barrett recalled how he found the body: a plump woman lying on her back, with her hands at her sides, tightly clenched. Her legs were spread open. Her clothes were disarranged, torn open at the front and turned up as far as the centre of the body, leaving the lower part of the body exposed. There was an absence of blood from her mouth, and no blood on the stairs leading to the landing.

According to Dr Timothy Killeen, who performed the post mortem examination at 5.30 on the morning of her discovery, Martha was middle-aged, 5ft 3in, plump, with dark hair and complexion. She was wearing a black bonnet, a long black jacket, a dark green skirt, brown petticoat, stockings and spring-sided boots which showed considerable wear.

Dr Killeen estimated Martha's time of death as approximately three hours before she was discovered, placing her death around 2.30am. He noted she had an

effusion of blood between the scalp and bone; the brain was pale but healthy; at least 22 stab wounds to the trunk; 17 in the breast, including 5 stab wounds to the left lung, 2 stabs to the right lung – albeit healthy, and the heart was stabbed once, which was rather fatty; except for stab wound nothing about the heart to cause death; some blood in the pericardium; the liver was healthy and stabbed 5 times; the spleen was healthy and stabbed twice; both kidneys were healthy; the stomach was healthy and stabbed 6 times; the intestines were healthy; the other organs were healthy; the lower portion of the body had one stab wound – 3" long and 1" deep, but was not mutilated; there was a lot of blood between her legs; nine stab wounds to the throat, yet it was not cut, and there was no evidence that the carotid arteries had been severed; the breasts, stomach, abdomen, and vagina seemed to have been the main areas; death was due to hemorrhage and loss of blood; sexual intercourse had not recently taken place; no evidence of a struggle; except for the wound on the chest bone, all injuries seem to have been inflicted by a right-handed person, using a penknife; the stab wound to the heart might have been made by a dagger or bayonet by a left-handed person.

Deputy Coroner Collier summed up and the jury returned a verdict of "Murdered by some person or persons unknown."

4.

POLLY NICHOLS

Mary Ann Walker, nicknamed Polly, the first of the so-called Canonical Five victims, was born on 26th August 1845 at Dawes Court, Shoe Lane off Fleet Street to Edward and Caroline. Her father was born on 15th December 1816 and died on September 1895, cause unknown. Her mother Caroline, née Webb, was born on 13th March 1822 and died on 29th November 1852 from phthisis. The burial record of 5th December 1852 showed that Caroline was living at Dean Street at the time of her death. Caroline and Edward were married on 17th February 1840 at Lambeth in South London. Polly had two brothers; Edward, born in 1844, and Frederick, born in 1849.

Reports at the time of Polly's murder described her as 5ft 2in tall, with brown eyes and brown hair turning grey. She had small, delicate features, with high cheekbones and a small scar on her forehead from a childhood injury. Five of her front teeth were reportedly missing.

In 1851, when aged six years old, Polly was living at 14 Dean Street in Soho with her parents and two brothers. Census takers had actually transcribed Edward Walker as 'Pollard Walters', and while Caroline and the children's forenames were taken correctly, they were also given the surname Walters. Edward was classed as a locksmith in this census, and Caroline gave her occupation as a launderess.

By 1861 Polly was living at 19 Harp Alley, St Bride in the City of London with her father, whose occupation was described as a 'smith' and engineer. Her brother Edward was also listed as an engineer. Youngest brother Frederick had died sometime between the 1851 and 1861 censuses.

On 16th July 1864 Polly married William Nichols at St Bride's Church. According to the marriage record both were of full age; William was a bachelor and Polly a spinster. Their residence was described only as 'St Bride', and William's occupation was recorded as 'Printer.' William's father was William Nichols Sr, and his occupation was given as 'Herald Printer.' Polly's father's occupation was listed as 'Blacksmith.'

Two years later, on July 4th 1866, Polly gave birth to their first child, Edward John Nichols. Her second son, George Percy, was born on 18th July 1868. Both Edward and Percy were baptised on 9th August 1868. Their home address was given as 131 Trafalgar Street. Alice Esther was born in 1870 (according to her later marriage certificate), and another daughter, Eliza Sarah, was born at the end of 1876. Polly's last child Henry Alfred Nichols was born at the end of 1878.

On 22nd April 1880 Polly was recorded as staying at the Newington Workhouse in Southwark. The record showed Mary Ann Nichols as being 35-years-old, her 'Calling or occupation' was simply noted as 'Laundry', and her response as to where she had slept the night before her admission was given as 'Wandsworth.' Under work done is 'Cleaning men's dormitories', and under the column 'Place where going' the answer given was 'Woolwich.'

A month later, on 31st May 1880, Polly was recorded again in the Newington Workhouse register. Her name was again given as Mary Ann Nichols, but this time her age had changed to 34. Her occupation was again given as 'Laundry', and she had slept the previous night at Woolwich. In the 'work done' column is noted 'Picking oakum'. Place going is just stated 'City.'

Picking oakum in Victorian times was an unpleasant and very monotonous task, and was usually used as a punishment in prison. The workhouses used it as a way to make the inmates pay for their keep.

Prisoners serving hard labour would cut used rope into two and then strike it with a mallet to remove the hard tar that coated it. Once this was done it was passed to those prisoners serving lesser sentences. They would then have to uncoil, unravel, unpick and shred the rope into fibres. According to the *Accounts and Papers of the House of Commons 1864*, at one workhouse each person had to pick at least ½lb of oakum in order to receive ½lb of bread in the morning. This could be withheld if the person refused to do the work. Performing this kind of labour shows the desperation of the people who went to the workhouse for food and shelter.

By 1880 William and Polly separated for the last time; they'd had a rocky relationship over the years and separated for short periods, but always reconciled. William blamed these separations on Polly. "The woman left me four or five times, if not six," he stated at her inquest.

At Polly's inquest her father claimed the breakup happened because William had had an affair with the nurse who helped with the birth of Henry Alfred. William didn't deny the affair, but he did say that it wasn't the reason for their separation, pointing out that he and Polly had stayed together another three years after the birth of Henry.

It's highly likely that the nurse Polly's father mentioned was Rosetta Walls née Vidler. In the 1881 census she was staying with her mother and siblings at 5 D Block Peabody Buildings, Lambeth. Rosetta was classed as married, but there was no sign of her husband Thomas. Living next door at 6 D Block Peabody Buildings in 1881 was William Nichols with his five children after retaining custody. By law William had to pay spousal support to Polly, and he paid 5s a week until 1882 when he proved in court that she was earning money by illicit means. William and Rosetta married two months after Polly's death, on 26th November 1888. William gave his occupation as a printer, and both he and Rosetta described themselves as widowers.

They had three children of their own: Arthur Nichols, who was born around 1882; Ethel M Nichols, born circa 1890; and Winifred Christine Nichols, born on 15th October 1892 and baptised on 4th November.

Over the next few years following her separation from William Polly was admitted to workhouses and infirmaries with regularity.

From 24th April 1882 to 18th January 1883 she was at Lambeth Workhouse; from 18th to 20th January 1883 she was at Lambeth Infirmary, and from 20th January to 24th March 1883 she returned to Lambeth Workhouse.

Between 24th March and 21st May 1883 Polly lived with her father in Camberwell. He testified at the inquest in 1888 that although not a sober person, she wasn't in the habit of staying out late at night. He admitted that her drinking caused friction between them as he was teetotal, but denied that he had thrown her out of his home, insisting she left the next morning of her own accord. While there is no reason to disbelieve him, we have to wonder why Polly went willingly into a workhouse, which was detested by the poor. It has to be asked why she felt this was more preferable than staying with her father.

It seems Polly went straight to Lambeth Workhouse, as her next record shows her admittance there from 21st May to 2nd June 1883.

In 1886 Edward John Nichols, Polly's eldest child, left his father William to go and live with his grandfather, Edward Walker. On 31st May that year Polly's brother Edward suffered severe burns when, in the process of retiring for the night, he was trying to extinguish a paraffin lamp which rested on his kitchen mantelpiece which consequently exploded. His hair caught fire and spread quickly to his chest and body. He was immediately rushed to hospital but died the following evening from shock and burns to his body. A verdict of accidental death was given. It was said that Mary Ann was respectably dressed when she went to his funeral.

Between 2nd June 1883 and 26th October 1887 Polly was said by her father to be living with one Thomas Drew, a blacksmith, with a shop in York Mews, 15 York Street in Walworth, South London.

On 25th October 1887 Polly spent one day in St Giles Workhouse on Endell Street. She then moved on, and records show that between 26th October to 2nd December 1887 she was at the Strand Workhouse in Edmonton, North London. From 2nd December to 19th December she went back to the Lambeth Workhouse, and from 4th January to 16th

April 1888 Polly was at Mitcham Workhouse and Holborn Infirmary.

From 16th April she was again at Lambeth Workhouse. However, this time was slightly different and Polly left the workhouse on 12th May to take a job as a domestic servant in the home of Samuel and Sarah Cowdry (née Manchee) at 26 Rose Hill Road, Wandsworth.

At the inquest into her death her father produced a letter she had sent him while at the Cowdrys. It read:

> *I just write to say you will be glad to know that I am settled in my new place, and going all right up to now. My people went out yesterday and have not returned, so I am left in charge. It is a grand place inside, with trees and gardens back and front. All has been newly done up. They are teetotalers and religious so I ought to get on. They are very nice people, and I have not too much to do. I hope you are all right and the boy has work. So goodbye for the present.*
>
> *From yours truly,*
>
> *Polly*
>
> *Answer soon, please, and let me know how you are.*

The boy Polly referred to was her eldest son Edward, who, as mentioned, had moved in with her father in 1886.

For reasons known only to Polly, she absconded from her job after just two months while her employers were on holiday, taking with her clothing worth £3 10s. It has been suggested that the fact that the Cowdrys were teetotallers caused a problem for Polly, who obviously liked a drink.

Polly found herself back at various workhouses and lodging houses. Until a few weeks before her death she had been living at Wilmott's Lodging House, a common lodging house at 18 Thrawl Street. She shared a room with four women, one of whom was Emily 'Nelly' Holland, who would later testify at Polly's inquest.

On 24th August 1888 Polly moved to another lodging house, the White House at 56 Flower and Dean Street, where men were allowed to share a bed with women – a practice frowned upon at many other lodging houses.

At 11.00pm on 30th August Polly was seen walking towards Whitechapel Road, and at 12.30am the following morning she was seen leaving The Frying Pan pub on the corner of Brick Lane and Thrawl Street. She was alone both times.

She was turned out of the kitchen of 18 Thrawl Street at 1.30am by the deputy of the lodging house as she didn't have the money needed for her bed. According to the deputy she wasn't too concerned, as she had acquired a new bonnet. She left with the words: "I'll soon get my doss money, look what a jolly bonnet I've got."

At approximately 2.30am she was seen on the corner of Osborn Street and Whitechapel Road by her roommate from 18 Thrawl Street, Emily Holland. Polly told her that she'd had her doss money three times already that evening, but had spent it all on drink. Emily later recalled how Polly was very drunk, and how she had tried to get her to go back to the lodging house with her. Polly however replied she would try one more attempt at earning some money before returning to 56 Flower and Dean Street.

After a few more minutes talking with Emily, Polly walked off down Whitechapel Road towards Buck's Row. This was the last time she was seen alive.

At approximately 3.40am, while walking to his job at Pickford's, Charles Allen Cross (aka Lechmere) passed down Buck's Row and saw on the other side of the road what he believed was an abandoned tarpaulin lying on the ground in front of a gated stable, about 150 yards from London Hospital.

At that moment another man, Robert Paul, who was on his way to his own work in Corbet's Court, Hanbury Street, travelled down Buck's Row when he saw Charles Cross standing in the middle of the road. Cross called him over and pointed to the body: "Come and look over here. There's a woman lying in the pavement."

As they both walked over to the body they saw Polly lying on her back with her clothes raised almost to her stomach. After feeling her cold hands Robert Paul believed she was dead, but as he pulled her clothing down he accidentally touched her breast and thought he felt movement.

PC Neil discovers the body of Polly Nichols in Buck's Row

He believed she was still breathing, but very lightly. Cross and Paul decided they needed to get to work and would report their discovery to the first police constable they saw.

At 3.45am PC Neil was walking his beat and making his way up Buck's Row when he came across Polly's body. It was only when shining his lantern on her that he realised the extent of her injuries:

> I found the deceased lying outside a gateway, her head turned towards the east. The gateway was closed. It was about nine or ten feet high, and led to some stables… Deceased was lying lengthways along the street, her left hand touching the gate. I examined the body by the aid of my lamp, and noticed blood oozing from a wound in the throat. She was lying on her back with her clothes disarranged. I felt her arm, which was quite warm from the joints upwards. Her eyes were wide open…

By this time PC Mizen, at the junction of Hanbury Street and Baker's Row, had been alerted to the discovery of the body by Cross and Paul.

Mizen made his way to the scene to find PC Neil and PC Thain already there. They decided to fetch Dr Rees Ralph Llewellyn from his surgery a short distance away. The surgeon gave a complete report as to Polly's injuries at the inquest, as reported in *The Times* of 1st September 1888:

> *On reaching Buck's Row I found the deceased lying flat on her back on the pathway, her legs being extended. Deceased was quite dead, and she had severe injuries to her throat. Her hands and wrists were cold, but her extremities were quite warm. Witness examined her chest and felt the heart. It was dark at the time. I believe she had not been dead more than half an hour. I am certain the injuries to the neck were not self-inflicted. There was very little blood around the neck, and there was no marks of any struggle or of blood, as though the body had been dragged. Witness gave the police directions to take the body to the mortuary, where he would make another examination...*

When at the mortuary Inspector Spratling lifted up Polly's clothing to note her injuries, it was first discovered that she had been disemboweled. Dr Llewellyn was sent for again, and recorded in his post-mortem report:

> *I found it to be that of a female about forty or forty-five years. Five of the teeth are missing, and there was a slight laceration of the tongue. There was a bruise running along the lower part of the jaw on the right hand side of the face. It might have been caused by a blow with a fist or pressure by the thumb. On the left side of the face there was a circular bruise, which also might have been done by the pressure of the fingers. On the left side of the neck, about a 1 in. below the jaw, there was an incision about 4in. in length, and ran from a point immediately below the ear. On the same side, but an inch below, and commencing about 1 in. in front of it, was a circular incision, which terminated at a point about 3 in. below the right jaw. That incision completely severed all the tissues down to the vertebrae. The large vessels of the neck on both sides were severed. The incision was about 8 in. in length. The cuts must have been caused by a long-bladed knife, moderately sharp, and used with great violence. No blood was found on the breast, either of the body or clothes. There were no injuries about the body until just about the lower part of the abdomen. Two*

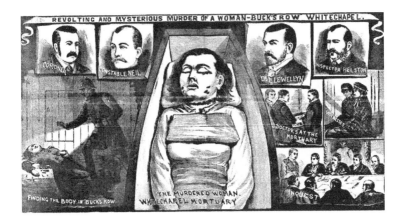

or three inches from the left side was a wound running in a jagged manner. The wound was a very deep one, and the tissues were cut through. There were several incisions running across the abdomen. There were also three or four similar cuts, running downwards, on the right side, all of which had been caused by a knife which had been used violently downwards. The injuries were from left to right, and might have been done by a left-handed person. All the injuries had been done by the same instrument.

At this stage Coroner Mr Wynne Baxter adjourned the inquiry until the following morning. After three more days of evidence and cross-examination the jury returned a verdict of "Wilful murder against some person or persons unknown."

5.

ANNIE CHAPMAN

Annie Eliza Smith, most commonly known as second Canonical victim Annie Chapman, was also known as 'Dark Annie' and Annie Siffey or Sivvey.

Although Annie was born into a working-class family, the daughter of George Smith and Ruth Chapman, it is said the family had a foothold in the 'middle-class bracket.' Her father was a private in the 2nd Regiment of the Queen's Life Guards, the mounted troops of the Household Cavalry Mounted Regiment tasked with guarding the official royal residences across Britain.

Annie was born in early September 1841, in Paddington. Her parents married a few months after her birth, on 22nd February 1842 at St James, Paddington. She had four younger siblings: Emily (b. 1844), Georgina (b.1856), Miriam (b.1858) and a brother born in 1861, whose name was recorded with a few variations: in the 1861 census he was recorded as 'Hamilton'; on his son's birth record he was listed as 'Fontin', and on his birth record he was registered as 'Fountain Hamilton'.

Annie's father George Smith died on 25th May 1866 at St George's Hospital, Hanover Square, from an ulcerated leg and exhaustion.

On 1st May 1869 Annie married John Alfred Chapman, a coachman, at All Saints Church and their address was given as 29 Montpelier Place,

Brompton. It appears that this was the address of Annie's mother, who lived there until her own death in 1893.

Annie gave birth to Emily Ruth Chapman on 25th June 1870, the family at that time living at 1 Brook Mews, Bayswater. On 5th June 1873 she gave birth to second daughter Annie Georgina Chapman, with the family now noted as living at 17 South Bruton Mews, Berkeley Square.

Not much is known in the ensuing years, but by now – according to sources – both John and Annie were apparently drinking heavily.

On 21st November 1880 her third child, John Alfred Chapman, was born. It appears John was not a healthy child, spending most of his life in the care of his grandmother and two aunts, Georgina and Emily. While it is noted in some accounts that John attended a charitable school outside Windsor where on occasion his mother would visit, it does appear that he was also in the care of other members of his family. The 1901 census records him as living with his aunts at 29 Montpelier Place, Westminster, where he's noted as being 'paralysed from infancy.' The 1911 census again has him living with his aunts at 29 Montpelier Place, and this time he is recorded as being 'paralysed from birth.'

According to the 1881 census, Annie and her three children Emily, Annie and John were recorded as visitors at the home of her mother at 29 Montpelier Place. Husband John Chapman was listed as Head of the household, although his household consisted of an apartment over the actual farm cottage owned by Mr Josiah Weeks, a farm bailiff at 41 St Leonard Farm Cottage, Clewer near Windsor. John was recorded as being married, with his occupation described as Coachman/Domestic servant.

Tragedy occurred for Annie and John when on 26th November 1882, at the age of twelve, Emily Ruth died of meningitis.

John and Annie separated in 1882, the cause, according to newspaper reports, being Annie's drunken and immoral ways. John continued living in Windsor while Annie moved back to London, earning a living crocheting antimacassars and selling flowers. John supplied her with an allowance of 10s a week, meaning Annie didn't have to resort to prostituting herself at that time.

By 1886 she was living with a sieve maker only known by the name John Sivvey at 30 Dorset Street in Spitalfields, a common lodging house. This explains Annie's being known by the names 'Sivvey' and 'Sievey' at times. When her income from husband John stopped without notice in early 1887, she learned from her brother-in-law, who lived in Oxford Street, Whitechapel, that John had died on Christmas Day 1886 from dropsy and cirrhosis of the liver – both alcohol-related illnesses. It was said by Annie's close friend Amelia Palmer that when Annie received the news of her estranged husband's death she became quite depressed and seemed to 'give up on life.' Not long after the sieve maker left her and moved to Notting Hill, implying he was only with her for her regular income.

Between May and June 1888 Annie moved to Crossingham's Lodging House at 35 Dorset Street. Here a double bed would cost 8d per night, or 4d a single. Inquest reports show that Annie had been in a relationship with a man known as 'The Pensioner', as he told people he was ex-army. This was proven false at Annie's inquest. His real name was Edward Stanley, a bricklayer's mate, and at the time of Annie's death he was living at 1 Osborn Place, Whitechapel and had never been in the army.

Timothy Donovan, the deputy of the Crossingham's lodging house, told the inquest how Edward would pay for Annie's bed on the condition she didn't take another man there. He also paid for the room of another lodger named Eliza Cooper. Edward stated he knew Annie in Windsor but this has yet to be corroborated.

Sometime in mid-August Annie met her brother Fountain on Commercial Road. She told him she was hard up, and he gave her two shillings. This was probably the last time he saw her alive.

On Saturday, 1st September Edward Stanley returned after being away since 6th August. He and Annie met at the corner of Brushfield Street.

Around this time Annie had a fight with lodger Eliza Cooper, her rival for Edward Stanley's affections, in The Britannia public house on the corner of Commercial Street and Dorset Street. It's not known exactly how, where and why the fight started as accounts are conflicting, but at some point Eliza Cooper struck Annie, causing a black eye and bruising

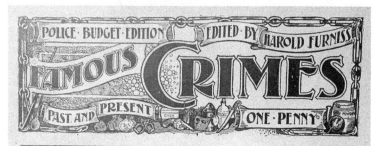

SHE HAD A ROW IN THE KITCHEN WITH ANOTHER WOMAN.

to her chest.

On Monday 3rd September Annie's friend Amelia Palmer saw her in Dorset Street. Amelia noticed the bruising on Annie's face and asked how she got it. This is when Annie told Amelia her version of her fight with Eliza, who claimed it was over an unreturned bar of soap. Annie stated that while an argument with Eliza did happen in The Britannia, the fight happened later at Crossingham's and it was over the fact that Annie had caught Eliza palming a florin from a friend of Edward Stanley named Harry the Hawker and replacing it with a penny. When Annie brought this to Harry's attention, Eliza struck her. Amelia said at the inquest that Annie had opened her dress to show her the bruising to her chest.

Regardless of the reason for the fight, it's clear that Annie came off worse, having sustained bruising to the chest and also to her eye and face.

The following day Annie and Amelia met up again, this time near Christ Church. Annie complained of feeling under the weather, commenting that she should go to the casual ward. While there's no record that she ever received medical attention, she did have medication on her at the time of her death. Palmer commented on her friend's pale complexion, and when Annie told her that she'd had nothing to eat or drink all that day Amelia gave her 2d and told her to buy some tea with it, not rum.

On Friday 7th September Palmer saw Annie in Dorset Street again. When she asked if she was going to Stratford, as she always did on a Friday to sell her wares, Annie said she was feeling too ill, but when Amelia returned to the spot a few minutes later Annie announced: "It is no use my giving way, I must pull myself together and go out and get some money or I shall have no lodgings."

Annie returned to Crossingham's lodging house at 11.30pm and asked permission to go to the kitchen. Just after midnight she was sharing a pint of beer with fellow lodger Frederick Stevens, who later described her as "Slightly the worse for wear." Another lodger, William Stevens, entered the kitchen a few minutes afterwards and Annie told him that she had gone to Vauxhall to visit her sister, who had given her money.

If this was the case then she spent it before getting back to Spitalfields, as she again had no money on her. Whether visiting her sister was an excuse to explain her travelling to Stratford to ply her trade, or Stevens was mistaken in what he'd heard can't be known, but researchers have so far found no record of Annie having any sisters living in Vauxhall at this time.

William Stevens also mentioned that Annie had told him she'd been to the hospital and had a bottle of lotion and a bottle of medicine. She took a box of pills from her pocket, at which point the box broke. Annie placed the pills in a piece of torn envelope she found on the floor. This envelope was later found on her body. Annie didn't have a bed for that night, however. Stevens mistakenly believed that she did, and so thought that she went up to her room not long after this to retire for the night. But in fact around 1.35am Annie returned to the lodging house kitchen to eat a baked potato. Her bottle of medicine from the casual ward was later found in room 29, the room she regularly kept when she had the money to pay for it. The simplest explanation was that she took that upstairs before going back out; this also implies that Annie had every intention of returning.

Donovan sent the night watchman, John Evans, for her doss money. Annie went to find Donovan and said "I haven't sufficient money for a bed, but don't let it. I shall not be long before I am in."

"You can find money for your beer but you can't find money for your bed," replied Donovan.

Annie simply said: "Never mind, Tim, I shall soon be back."

Donovan stated at the inquest that he thought Annie was drunk.

Evans escorted Annie outside. She told him, "I won't be long Brummy, see that Tim keeps the bed for me." Annie walked down Little Paternoster Street and turned right into Brushfield Street, towards Spitalfields Church. Evans also thought Annie was worse for drink. This would be the last time he saw her alive.

On Monday 10th September John Davis, a carman living at 29 Hanbury Street, got up at approximately 5.45am and went straight out to the yard, probably to use the outside toilet. He was certain of the time because he heard the bell of the Spitalfields church strike. When he descended the steps into the yard he saw the body of a woman lying flat on her back between steps and the fence which separated the yard from that of No. 27. He ran back into the house and out the front door into Hanbury Street, where he met James Kent, James Green and Henry Holland and told them of the gruesome discovery. Davis then went to Commercial Street Police Station to inform the police.

As the first witness at the subsequent inquest, he stated that he had never seen the deceased before, although he had only lived at 29 Hanbury Street for a fortnight.

Second in the witness box was Amelia Palmer, who said she had lived at 30 Dorset Street for the past four years. She revealed quite a few 'facts' given to her by Annie. Amelia had known Annie for a few years, when they both lived at 30 Dorset Street. She informed the inquest that Annie formerly lived in Windsor, and was the widow of Frederick [sic] Chapman, a veterinary surgeon [sic], who died about 18 months previously. She had two children who were sent away to school when her husband died. Annie had spoken of a mother and sister, though Amelia didn't think they were on friendly terms.

According to what she'd told Amelia, Annie had been separated from her husband for four years or more, and she had since lived at different common lodging houses in the neighbourhoods of Spitalfields and Whitechapel. Annie moved from 30 Dorset Street about two years previously and began living with the man who made iron sieves. At this point she was still receiving 10s a week allowance from her husband. Amelia acknowledged that Annie was in the habit of staying out late at night, and that she wasn't very particular in what she did to earn her money. Amelia said she was in the habit of going to Stratford. In Amelia's opinion Annie was an 'industrial' and clever woman.

The deputy of the common lodging house at 35 Dorset Street, Timothy Donovan, stated that he had seen the body in the mortuary and believed it was the woman who had been lodging at his place for about four months, but she hadn't been there any day of the previous week until the Friday. He said that at 7.00pm on Friday 7th September Annie had gone

THE REAR OF 29, HANBURY STREET.
(The + shows where the body was found.)

to the lodging house and asked to be allowed into the kitchen. When he had enquired about her whereabouts all week she had explained that she'd been to the infirmary.

Donovan recalled Annie had stayed in the kitchen until about 2.00am the next morning, when she'd asked him to keep her bed for her as she didn't have her doss money, but she would go out and get it and wouldn't be long. He stated he had never had any trouble with Annie, who he said was always on friendly terms with all the other lodgers. He confirmed that he had seen The Pensioner at the lodging house, and while he didn't know his name he gave the description of a man 45-years-old, about 5ft 8in height. At times he would have the appearance of a dock labourer and other times his appearance was of something better.

Day two of the inquest took place on Wednesday 12th September. John Richardson was one of the people to give his testimony. He stated that at 4.45am he entered the backyard of 29 Hanbury Street on his way to work. It was his mother's house, but due to recent thefts he tended to go and check that the property was secure. After standing at the back steps and looking over to see the lock on the cellar door, he sat down on the steps to remove a piece of leather from his boots. Although quite dark, he was sitting no more than a yard away from where Annie's head would have been had her body been there at that time. He later testified he saw nothing of out of the ordinary.

Dr George Bagster Phillips' testimony was given on day three of the inquest, 13th September. While we don't have the original postmortem report from Dr Phillips at the inquest the account is recorded and reported in the *Daily Telegraph*. On the 3rd day of the inquest, 13th September 1888 (published in the newspaper on the 14th) Dr Phillips described how he arrived in the back yard of 29 Hanbury Street at 6.30 am and observed the body of a female lying on her back, at the left side of the steps which lead from the passage:

> *The head was about 6 in. in front of the level of the bottom step, and her feet were towards a shed, which proved to contain wood, at the bottom of the yard. The left arm was placed across the left breast. The legs were drawn up, the feet resting on the ground, and the knees*

turned outwards. The face was swollen and turned on the right side. The tongue protruded between the front teeth, but not beyond the lips. The tongue was evidently much swollen. The front teeth were perfect, so far as the first molar, top and bottom and very fine teeth they were. The body was terribly mutilated. He searched the yard, and in doing so found a small piece of coarse muslin and a pocket comb in a paper case lying at the feet of the woman near the paling; and they apparently had been placed there in order or arranged there. He also found and delivered to the police other articles, including the leather apron. The stiffness of the limbs was not marked but was evidently commencing. He noticed that the throat was dissevered deeply; that the incisions through the skin were jagged, and reached right round the neck. On the back wall of the house, between the steps and the paling which bounded the yard on the left side, about 18in. from the ground, where about six patches of blood, varying in size from a sixpenny piece to a small point. On the wooden paling, between the yard in question, and the next, smears of blood, corresponding to where the head of the deceased lay, were to be seen. These were about 14 in. from the ground, and immediately above the part where the blood lay that had flowed from the neck.

…The instrument used at the throat and abdomen was the same. It must have been a very sharp knife, with a thin, narrow blade and must have been at least 6 in. to 8 in. in length, probably longer. He should say that the injuries could not have been inflicted by a bayonet or a sword bayonet. They could have been done by such an instrument as a medical man used for post mortem purposes, but the ordinary surgical cases might not contain such an instrument. Those used by slaughter-men, well ground down, might have caused them. He thought the knives used by those in the leather trade would not be long enough in the blade. There were indications of anatomical knowledge, which were only less indicated in consequence of haste. The whole body was not present, the absent portions being from the abdomen. The mode in which these portions were extracted showed some anatomical knowledge. He did not think these portions were lost in the transit of the body. He should say that the deceased had been dead at least two hours, and probably more, when he first saw her; but it was right to mention that it was a fairly cool morning, and

that the body would be more apt to cool rapidly from it's having lost a great quantity of blood. There was no evidence about the body of the woman of a struggle having taken place. He was positive the deceased entered the yard alive..."

At this point Dr Phillips stopped his testimony to complain about the inadequate facilities he and his colleagues had to use for their post-mortem examinations. He felt the 'shed' they had to use was a great disadvantage in how they did their jobs. He also was reluctant to give all the details of the injuries that had been inflicted on Annie, feeling the cause of death should be enough for public record. The Coroner, Wynne Baxter, agreed to have the details of Annie's cause of death for now and further details postponed to a later date if they were needed. Phillips then continued with his findings from his post-mortem report:

He noticed the same protrusions of the tongue. There was a bruise over the right temple. On the upper eyelid there was a bruise, and there were two distinct bruises, each the size of a man's thumb, on the forepart of the top of the chest. The stiffness of the limbs was now well marked. There was a bruise over the middle part of the bone of the right hand. There was an old scar on the left frontal bone. The stiffness was more noticeable on the left side, especially in the fingers, which were partly closed. There was an abrasion over the ring finger, with distinct markings of a ring or rings. The throat had been severed, as before described. The incisions into the skin indicated that they had been made from the left side of the neck. There were two distinct, clean cuts on the left side of the spine. They were parallel from each other and separated by about half an inch. The muscular structures appeared as though an attempt had been made to separate the bones of the neck. There were various mutilations to the body, but he was of the opinion that they occurred subsequent to the death of the woman, and to the large escape of blood from the division of the neck...

The deceased was far advanced in disease of the lungs and membranes of the brain, but they had nothing to do with the cause of death. The stomach contained a little food, but there was not any sign of fluid. There was no appearance of the deceased having taken alcohol, but there were signs of great deprivation, and he should say she had been badly fed. He was convinced she had not taken any strong alcohol for some hours before her death. The injuries were certainly not self-inflicted. The bruises on the face were evidently recent, especially about the chin and side of the jaw, but the bruises in front of the chest and temple were of longer standing – probably of days. He was of the opinion that the person who cut the deceased's throat took hold of her by the chin, and then commenced the incision from left to right. He thought it was highly probable that a person could call out, but with regard to an idea that she might have been gagged he could only point to the swollen face and the protruding tongue, both of which were signs of suffocation.

Dr Phillips was recalled on 19th September and begrudgingly gave a more detailed account of the injuries from the post-mortem after the coroner had decided these details were indeed needed:

The abdomen had been entirely laid open, the intestines severed from their mesenteric attachments, had been lifted out of the body and placed on the shoulder of the corset. Whilst from the pelvis, the uterus and its appendages with the upper portion of the vagina and the posterior two thirds of the bladder, had been entirely removed. No trace of these parts could be found and the incisions were cleanly cut, avoiding the rectum and dividing the vagina low enough to avoid injury to the cervix uteri. Obviously the work of an expert – of one, at least who had such knowledge of anatomical or pathological examinations as to be enabled to secure the pelvic organs with one sweep of the knife, which must therefore have been at least 5 or 6 inches in length, probably more. The appearance of the cuts confirmed him in the opinion that the instrument, like the one that had divided the neck, had been of a very sharp character. The mode in which the knife had been used seemed to indicate great anatomical knowledge.

Dr Phillips thought that he himself could not have performed all the injuries described, even without a struggle, in under a quarter of an hour. If he had done it in a deliberate way such as would fall to the duties of a surgeon, it probably would have taken him the best part of an hour.

Day four of the inquest was held on Wednesday 19th September, and included the testimonies of witnesses Elizabeth Long and Albert Cadosch.

Elizabeth Long recalled that she saw Annie with a man near to 29 Hanbury Street while she was on her way to work. She was confident of the time as being 5.30am, as she heard the clock on the Black Eagle Brewery in nearby Brick Lane strike the half hour as she'd turned into Hanbury Street. She stated the man and woman were talking, and that she heard the man say "Will you?" to which the woman replied "Yes."

Chapman had her back towards Spitalfields Market, and was thus facing Long. As the man had his back to her, Elizabeth Long didn't see the man's face but noticed he was dark and wearing a brown low-crowned felt hat and dark coat. He appeared to be a man of around forty years of age and a little taller than the deceased's five feet. She felt the woman she saw was the deceased.

Testimony was given by Albert Cadosch, a young carpenter who resided next door to 29 Hanbury Street at No. 27. He went into the backyard at about a quarter to five in the morning. On returning to the house at approximately 5.15am he heard a voice say "No." Albert didn't believe it was from his own yard, but felt that it came from the yard of No. 29. He did admit that it could have come from either side of the yard to No. 27. After going indoors and returning outside a few minutes later, he said he'd heard something fall against the fence which divided his yard from that of No. 29. He admitted that he didn't think to look over the fence, which he estimated to be between 5ft 6in and 6ft in height, as he was thinking about his work and just assumed it was noise made by his neighbours who were packing-case makers.

After five days the Coroner Mr Wynne Baxter summed up the case, and the inquest was closed with the final declaration of "Wilful murder against a person or person unknown."

6.

LIZ STRIDE

Elizabeth Gustafsdotter, more commonly known as Liz Stride but also apparently called 'Long Liz' and 'Hippy Lip Annie', was born on 27th November 1843 on a farm at Stora Tumlehed in Torslanda, Sweden, to parents Gustaf Ericsson and Beata Carsldotter. She was baptised on 5th December 1843.

She had three siblings: Anna Christina Ericsson (b.1840), Lars Bernhard Gustafsson (b.1848) and Svante (b.1851). By 1860 Elisabeth had moved to Gothenburg, and in 1861 was in the employ of Lars Fredrik Olofsson as a domestic servant.

On 25th August 1864 Liz's mother Beata died. A couple of months later, in the October, Liz was noted as living in Philgaten in Ostra Haga, a suburb of Gothenburg. In March 1865 Liz was registered as a prostitute with the Gothenburg police and the following month on 21st April she gave birth to a stillborn girl. Between October and November that year she was treated in Kurhuset for venereal disease. The hospital entry made on 17th October showed she was treated for a venereal ulcer and again on 3rd November, although the description this time was just 'venereal disease.' Kurhuset hospital records show Liz had to be examined on 3rd, 7th, 10th and 14th November. She was now healthy, and would no longer have to report to the Police.

Governments worldwide passed laws in the 1700s that tried to contain and eradicate venereal diseases, especially syphilis, that were spreading at an alarming rate. Sweden's laws were originally aimed at all citizens within certain social and occupational groups, but a law introduced in 1813 saw women specifically targeted, with the result that any woman employed in certain jobs such as working in a restaurant, pub or inn, as well as being a 'loose woman' who might be suspected of spreading a venereal disease, could be forcibly stopped and medically examined. From 1859 a prostitute would be examined weekly, and failure to adhere to this law could be punishable by up to one year's hard labour. In 1864 there was reform in this penal code which grounded regulationism in the vagrancy law, although not universally across Sweden until 1918.

While not entirely sure which account is correct, it is said that Liz's mother died on 25th August 1864 but her estate wasn't settled until January 1867, leaving Liz 65 Swedish krona in her will, or that after her mother's death the family moved away from the home and in 1865 her father sold the house to her mother's brother Lars Carlson, from which all the children received a lump sum of money.

Whatever, the reason the money enabled Liz to move away from her life in Sweden and on 7th February 1866 she arrived in London after submitting a new certificate of altered residence. On 10th July she registered as an unmarried woman at the Swedish Church, Prince's Square, Stepney.

Liz married John Thomas Stride on 7th March 1869. She was recorded as a spinster of 'full age', and the address she gave at the time was 67 Gower Street. Her father was recorded as Augustus Gustafson, a labourer. John Stride was recorded as a bachelor of 'full age' – in fact he was 20 years her senior. A ship's carpenter, his address was noted as 21 Munster Street, Regent's Park. His father was William Stride, a shipwright.

Some time after the marriage in 1869 the couple opened a coffee shop. At the inquest both Michael Kidney and Charles Preston commented that Liz had told them she ran a coffee house with her husband in Chrisp Street, Poplar, but they must not have stayed long at this address as in the Post Office London Directory John Thomas Stride's name is found at

Upper North Street East, on the east side situated between Caledonian Road and Grundy Street. It is noted in two records in the Post Office Directory as both a coffee house and also coffee rooms.

By the 1871 census, however, they had moved again and were now running a coffee shop business at 178 Poplar High Street. According to some accounts, they were living away from the business premises and resided a few doors away at 172 High Street, however this seems unlikely as there isn't actually a No. 172 on the census in 1871.

According to the 1875 *London Directory* this business had been taken over by a Mr John Dale that year, so for some unknown reason Liz and John were no longer running coffee shops and it is highly likely that John had resumed his trade as a carpenter, if in fact, he ever stopped. It's conceivable to think that while John's name is on the records for the coffee houses, it was more than likely to assume Liz ran them while he continued with his carpentry.

On 21st March 1877 Liz was remanded at Thames Magistrates' Court and sent to Poplar workhouse, being taken there by the police. There is no record of where John was at this time.

The 1881 census showed the couple living at 69 Usher Row in Bow, with John still working as a carpenter and Liz with no recorded occupation. He was 54-years-old and Liz 34. Her place of birth was noted as Stockholm, Sweden, with 'British subject' written underneath.

From 28th December 1881 to 4th January 1882 Liz was treated at the Whitechapel Union Infirmary for bronchitis. After leaving the Infirmary she went straight to Whitechapel workhouse, having separated from her husband, the marriage not being able to stand the strain of her drinking. From this date until her death Liz had no fixed place of residence, instead frequenting common lodging houses.

On 24th October 1884 John Stride died from heart disease at Stepney Sick Asylum.

The following year Liz met Michael Kidney, a dockside labourer who was seven years her junior, and they lived together on and off until her death, mainly residing in lodging houses in Devonshire Street. Liz reportedly left Michael on numerous occasions, their relationship described as a stormy one. It was said that he tried to lock her in with a padlock, but she always managed to escape. In fact, what looked like a padlock key was found in Liz's possession at the time of her death, which could explain her 'escapes.'

Liz received alms from the Swedish Church on 20th and 23rd May 1886. The Clerk of the Church, Sven Olsson, would later recall. He noted that her address at the time was recorded as Devonshire Street.

In March 1887 Liz was registered as an inmate of Poplar Workhouse. The following month she accused Michael Kidney of assault, although the charges were dropped when she failed to appear in court. Liz herself appeared before magistrates a total of eight times for convictions of drunkenness. In July 1888 Kidney was sent to jail for three days for being drunk and disorderly and using obscene language. On both 15th and 20th September that year Liz again received aid from the Swedish Church.

Michael Kidney later stated at the inquest that the last time he saw Liz was on Tuesday 25th September. He expected her to be there when he returned home from work, but she had left. He said he wasn't concerned: "It was drink that made her go away. She always returned without me going after her. I think she liked me better than any other man."

The following day, on the 26th, Liz was now lodging at 32 Flower and Dean Street. She hadn't been there in the previous three months and told another lodger, Catherine Lane, that she'd had words with the man she was living with. Elizabeth Tanner, the lodging house deputy, would also state that Liz had moved there after having a quarrel with Kidney.

Eyewitness accounts of Liz Stride's last hours allow a little insight into her life.

The afternoon of 29th September saw her cleaning two rooms of her lodging house, for which Elizabeth Tanner paid her sixpence. At 6.30pm Liz was seen enjoying a drink in the nearby Queen's Head, but by 7.00pm had returned to the lodging house to clean herself up. This was verified by fellow lodgers Charles Preston, from whom she'd asked for a loan of a clothes brush, and Catherine Lane, to whom Liz gave a piece of green velvet trim and asked her to keep until she returned.

At 7.30pm Liz had again left the lodging house, and the next sighting of her was to be at 11.00pm when J. Best and John Gardner believed they saw her in the doorway of the Bricklayer's Arms at 34 Settles Street. They stated she was in the company of a man about 5ft 5in tall with a black moustache, sandy eyelashes and who was wearing a black morning suit with a billycock hat. They were sheltering from the rain in a doorway, before hurrying off towards Commercial Road.

Approximately 11.45pm Morris Eagle left the International Working Men's Educational Club on Berner Street to walk his young lady to her home.

At around the same time, a labourer by the name of William Marshall was standing outside his lodging house at 64 Berner Street when he noticed a man and a woman outside on the pavement opposite No. 68, between Christian Street and Boyd Street. The couple moved off up the road in the direction of Dutfield's Yard. Marshall described the man as middle-aged, stout and having the appearance of a clerk. He was about 5ft 6in tall, clean shaven and respectably dressed. He wore a small black cutaway coat, dark trousers and a round cap with a sailor-like peak.

Nearly an hour later, at 12.35am on 30th September 1888, PC William Smith was walking his beat along Berner Street when he noticed a man and a woman at the opposite side of the road to Dutfield's Yard, where Liz would be later found. PC Smith's description was of a man 28 years of age, 5ft 7in tall and wearing a dark overcoat, a hard felt deerstalker, dark overcoat and clothing. He noted that the woman was sporting a flower on her jacket.

Morris Eagle returned to the Club around 12.35am and, discovering the front door locked, went through the gates into Dutfield's Yard and entered the club by the side door. He told the inquest he saw nothing, and would have probably noticed a man and a woman had they been standing in the yard, or a woman lying on the ground yards away from where he entered the gates, although as it was so dark he felt he couldn't say for certain.

At 12.45am James Brown of 35 Fairclough Street left his home in order to get some supper. Heading towards a chandler's shop on the corner of Fairclough Street and Berner Street, as he crossed the road he saw the couple standing by the Board School on Fairclough Street. As he passed them he heard the woman say, "No, not tonight, some other night." At the inquest Brown would say that he didn't notice any foreign accent in her voice, but the comment made him turn round and look at the couple. He was certain that the woman he saw was Elizabeth Stride, although he said that he didn't notice any flowers on her dress. The man was standing with his arm up against the wall and the woman had her back to the wall, facing him. He was wearing a long overcoat which almost came down to his heels. Brown estimated him to be about 5ft 7in in height and had a 'stoutish' build. Both people appeared sober. It wasn't raining at the time.

At approximately the same time Israel Schwartz, a Jew who had just moved to England and spoke no English, turned into Berner Street as he headed to his lodgings on Ellen Street off Back Church Lane, when he noticed a man walking ahead of him. The man stopped to talk to a woman who was standing in the gateway of Dutfield's Yard. He attempted to pull the woman into the street, but then turned her around and threw her to the ground. Schwartz heard the woman scream three times, but not very loudly. Feeling this was a domestic quarrel that he didn't want to be involved with, Schwartz crossed to the opposite side of the street. It was at this point that he saw another man standing on the opposite side of the street, lighting a pipe.

The man accosting the woman called out "Lipski", although Schwartz wasn't sure if this was to the man with the pipe or himself. The word 'Lipski' had been used as a racial slur since the murder of Miriam Angel the previous year by Israel Lipski in nearby Batty Street.

Schwartz realised that the man with the pipe was now walking behind him. Fearing that he was also going to be attacked, he ran as far as the railway arch, where he saw that the man was no longer following him. Later, Schwartz was emphatic that the woman he saw at the mortuary was Elizabeth Stride.

His description of the man with the woman was that he was 5ft 5in tall, around 30-years-old, with dark hair and a small brown moustache. He had a full face with a fair complexion and broad shoulders. He seemed to be slightly intoxicated.

The man with the pipe was described as 5ft 11in, 35-years-old with a fresh complexion and light brown hair. He was wearing a dark overcoat and an old black hard felt hat with a wide brim. He was holding a clay pipe in his hands. Although his apparent following of Schwartz was alarming, a report by Chief Inspector Swanson dated 19th October 1888 stated: "The police apparently do not suspect the second man." So it seems that he was for some reason cleared from enquiries.

Surprisingly, Israel Schwartz didn't attend the inquest. Whether this was because the police felt his evidence wasn't relevant to the murder or wanted to keep his evidence quiet is not known. However, in a report by Chief Inspector Swanson dated 19th October he stated that "If Schwartz is to be believed, and the police report of his statement casts no doubt on it, it follows if they are describing different men…" So it can be said for certain that, at the very least, early on in the investigation the police believed the validity of Schwartz's statement.

At 1.00am Louis Diemshitz, a costermonger and Steward of the International Working Men's Educational Club, returned to Berner Street after a day selling jewellery at a local market. As he turned his pony and cart into Dutfield's Yard, the gates being wide open, his pony shied to the left and wouldn't go any further forward. As it was in almost complete darkness at this point, the light from the Club's windows barely reaching this far, Diemshitz prodded around to his right with his whip at an unidentifiable object laying on the ground. He crouched and lit a match to see if he could identify the object. The match flared for mere seconds, but it was enough for him to realise the object was in fact a woman. Not sure if she was just drunk or indeed dead, Diemshitz hurried inside for a candle, telling his wife and others still in the Club about the body lying outside. Returning to the yard with the lit candle and colleagues Isaac Kozebrodsky and Morris Eagle, Diemshitz immediately saw that her throat had been cut and that blood was slowly beginning to stain the cobbles around her.

Eagle ran for the police. Reaching the corner of Commercial Street

THE FIFTH VICTIM of the WHITECHAPEL FIEND.

and Christian Street he came across two police officers, who returned to Dutfield's Yard with him.

One of the constables, PC Lamb, made sure the gathering crowd kept their distance, then turned his lamp on the body and knelt down to touch her face – it was still warm. He felt her wrist, but there was no pulse. The blood which has flowed from the wound to the throat had flowed towards the Club's door, and Lamb noticed that it was still liquid. The blood around Liz's throat was now partially congealed. He noticed that her clothes were not in disarray, with no apparent attempt to raise them and mutilate the body. He made sure no-one touched the body.

PC Lamb sent Eagle to Leman Street Police Station and then sent for Dr Blackwell of nearby 100 Commercial Road, who arrived at 1.15am. The doctor noted that the deceased had been found lying on her left side, facing towards the right wall of the Club. Her legs were drawn up slightly towards her chest, her feet close to the wall. Her head was resting just past a carriage wheel rut, her neck over said rut. Her dress was unfastened at the neck. Her neck, chest and legs were still quite warm, whereas her face was slightly warm. Her hands, however, were cold, the right open and lying on her chest. The left hand, which was on the ground, was partially closed and still held a small packet of cachous, wrapped in tissue paper.

Dr George Bagster Phillips arrived at the scene at 1.20am after being summoned to the Leman Street Police Station from his home at 2 Spital Square. From there he was taken to Berner Street. His description of how the body was found was very similar to that of Dr Blackwell's, the only real discernible difference in the accounts being that Phillips noted that not only were cachous found in Liz's left hand, but a number were also found in the gutter.

At 4.30am the body was moved to St-George's-in-the-East mortuary and by 5.00am, after detectives had concluded their search of the scene, PC Albert Collins had washed the blood away from the yard, leaving no sign of the atrocity that had been committed there.

The inquest was opened by Wynne Baxter at the Vestry Hall in Cable Street on Monday 1st October, hearing testimony from various witnesses.

Michael Kidney, the man Liz had been living with at 38 Dorset Street until just shortly before her death, was called to give evidence. He refuted the fact that he and Liz had quarrelled the day before she left. Surprisingly, even though two separate witnesses had confirmed this the courts didn't push Kidney on the matter. He admitted that he and Liz had quarrelled at times, blaming it on her drinking, but said that she would always go back to him, so he wasn't concerned when she left on occasions.

Another witness called was Sven Olsson, who resided at 36 Prince's Square. As Clerk to the Swedish Church he was able to give information on Liz's life before moving to Spitalfields from the Church registers. He stated that he had known the deceased for 17 years, and confirmed that she was a Swedish woman, her maiden name being Elizabeth Gustafsdotter. She was wife to John Thomas Stride, a ship's carpenter, and was born on 27th November 1843 at Torslanda, Sweden. Olsson confirmed that Liz was registered at the Church on 19th July 1866, and that she was registered at that time as an unmarried woman.

Sven Olsson went on to say that Liz had informed the Church that her husband had drowned in the *Princess Alice* disaster.

The SS *Princess Alice*, formerly PS *Bute*, was a paddle steamer. While sailing on the Thames on 3rd September 1878 she was in a collision with a cargo ship, *The Bywell Castle*, off Tripcock Point. The *Princess Alice* sank in just four minutes, and six hundred and fifty lives were lost.

Liz had told this story to quite a few people; in some versions she also told of the loss of her children in the disaster. As John died in Stepney Sick Asylum and we have no record of her having any children, it seems more than likely that Liz fabricated these stories to elicit sympathy and financial aid from the Church.

Also included within the inquest testimonies was the result of the post mortem conducted by Dr George Bagster Phillips:

At 3pm on Monday, at St George's mortuary, in the presence of Dr Rygate and Mr Johnston, Dr Blackwell and I made a post mortem examination. Dr Blackwell kindly consented to make the dissection. Rigor Mortis was still thoroughly marked. There was mud on the left side of the face and it was matted in the head. We then removed the clothes. The body was fairly nourished. Over both shoulders, especially the right, and under the collar-bone and in front of the chest there was a blueish discolouration, which I have watched and have seen on two occasions since. There was a clean-cut incision on the neck. It was 6in. in length and commenced 2½ in. in a straight line below the angle of the jaw, ¾ in. over an undivided muscle, and then, becoming deeper, dividing the sheath. The cut was very clean, and deviated a little downwards. The artery and other vessels contained in the sheath were all cut through. The cut through the tissues on the right side was more superficial, and tailed off to about 2 in. below the right angle of the jaw. The deep vessels on that side were uninjured. From this it was evident that the haemorrhage was caused through the partial severance of the left carotid artery. Decomposition had commenced in the skin. Dark brown spots were on the anterior surface of the left chin. There was a deformity in the bones of the right leg, which was not straight, but bowed forwards. There was no recent external injury save to the neck. The body being washed more thoroughly, I could see some healing sores. The lobe of the left ear was torn as if from the removal or wearing through of an earring, but it was thoroughly healed. On removing the scalp there was no sign of bruising or extravasation of blood. The skull was about a sixth of an inch in thickness, and the brain was fairly normal. The left lung had old adhesions to the chest wall, the right slightly. Both lungs were unusually pale. There was no fluid in the pericardium. The heart was small, the left ventricle firmly contracted and the right slightly so. There was no clot in the pulmonary artery, but the right ventricle was full of dark clot.

The left was firmly contracted so as to be absolutely empty. The stomach was large, and the mucous membrane only congested. It contained partly-digested food, apparently consisting of cheese, potato and a farinaceous powder. All the teeth on the lower jaw were absent. On Tuesday I again went to the mortuary to observe the marks on the shoulder. I found it in the pocket of the underskirt of the deceased the following articles – Key as if belonging to a padlock, a small piece of lead pencil, a pocket comb, a broken piece of comb, a metal spoon, some buttons and a hook. Examining her jacket, I found that, while there was a small amount of mud on the right side, the left was well plastered with mud. I have not see the two pocket handkerchiefs.

When the coroner enquired as to the actual cause of death, Dr Phillips answered that it was undoubtedly from the loss of blood from the left carotid artery and division of the windpipe.

The Times of 6th October 1888 reported that Dr Phillips was recalled to give further evidence:

After the last examination in company with Dr Blackwell and Dr Brown, I went to the mortuary and examined more carefully the roof of the mouth. I could not find any injury to or absence of anything from the mouth. I have also carefully examined the two handkerchiefs and have not found any blood on them. I believe the stains on the larger one were fruit stains. I am convinced that the deceased had not swallowed either skin or seed of a grape within many hours of her death. The abrasion which I spoke of on the right side of the neck was only apparently an abrasion, for on washing it the staining was removed and the skin was found to be uninjured. The knife was produced on the last occasion was submitted to me by Constable 282 H. On examination I found it to be such a knife as would be used in a chandler's shop, called a slicing knife. It had blood upon it, which was similar to that of a warm blooded being. It has been recently blunted and the edge turned by apparently rubbing on a stone. It was evidently before that a very sharp knife. Such a knife could have produced the incision and injuries to the neck of the deceased, but it was not such a weapon as I would have chosen to inflict injuries in this particular place; and if my opinion as regards to the position of the body is correct, the knife in question would become an improbable instrument as having caused the incision.

After a short deliberation, the jury returned a verdict of "Wilful murder against some person or persons unknown."

7

CATHERINE EDDOWES

Catherine Eddowes was born on 14th April 1842 at Graiseley Green, Wolverhampton. She was part of a big family whose lives can be tracked using the records from the time.

Her father George Eddowes was a tin plate worker from Wolverhampton. While we don't have his birth details, we know that he was baptized on 1st August 1808 at Bilston, Staffordshire to parents Thomas and Mary Eddowes. He married Catherine Evans on 13th August 1832 at St Mary's Church at Bushbury in Staffordshire, although his surname is noted on the marriage certificate incorrectly as 'Hedowes'.

They had twelve children: Alfred (born circa 1832), Harriet (b.1833), Emma (b.1834), Eliza (b.1837), Elizabeth (b.1839), Thomas (born 9th December 1844), George (born 19th October 1846), John (born c.1849), Sarah Ann (b.1850), Mary Ann (b.1852) and William, who was born on 22nd July 1854 in Bermondsey. Sadly, according to death records William died just a few months later on the 9th December 1854.

The 1841 census showed Catherine's parents living at Graiseley Green, with Alfred, Harriet, Emma and Elizabeth. In 1843 the Eddowes family moved to Bermondsey in south London, and by the 1851 census were living at 35 West Street in Bermondsey, although Alfred, Harriet and Emma had now moved away and were married.

Catherine's mother died of phthisis on 17th November 1855 at 7 Winter's Square, Bermondsey, and about two years later father George also passed away. His signature on his daughter Elizabeth's marriage certificate was dated 21st September 1857, so his death must have been after this date.

By 1861 Catherine had returned to Wolverhampton and was now living with her Uncle William Eddowes and his family at 50 Bilston Street, according to the 1861 census. The entry records her occupation as a 'scourer.' Around this time she met Thomas Conway, a pensioner who had served in the 18th Irish Regiment, and on 18th April 1863 Catherine gave birth to their daughter Catherine Ann (known as Annie) in the Yarmouth Workhouse Norfolk. In 1868 Catherine gave birth to her second child, Thomas Conway, at Westminster.

By 1871 the family were living at 1 Queen Street, St-George-the-Martyr Southwark , where Thomas was recorded as a pedlar and Catherine a laundress. Both children were listed as scholars.

In 1873 Catherine gave birth to her third child, Alfred George Conway, in Middlesex. In the Register of Births in the St-George-the-Martyr Workhouse, St Saviours Union on 14th August 1873 a 'male' was born to Kate Conway and 'unknown'. Kate had been admitted from St-George-the-Martyr.

In the England and Wales Civil register an Alfred George Conway was born in the third quarter of 1873 in St Saviour. It is likely this is the son of Catherine, although it does appear he used his middle name of George throughout most of his life.

An entry in the Greenwich Workhouse records of Tuesday 9th November 1876 noted Kate Eddowes as a 'hawker removable', a Roman Catholic aged 34. With her were Catherine Jr aged 13, Thomas Jr, 8 and Alfred, 2. Their address was recorded as 4 Giffen Street.

Although we haven't been able to locate the records for the family in the discharge record for the Greenwich workhouse on Woolwich Road, dated 17th November 1876, there is a record of Catherine Eddowes, aged 13 and Thomas Eddowes, aged 8 going to 'Sutton'. As all the other names that were 'Going to Sutton' on that page were under the age of 15, it seems likely they were all going to a school based in Sutton.

Another son, Frederick William Eddowes, was born in the first quarter of 1877 in Greenwich. A workhouse report lists Frederick as an 8-month-old child, admitted along with his mother, Catherine Eddowes, to the Greenwich workhouse, Woolwich Road on 17th October 1877. The admission entry states that Catherine Eddowes was a hawker at Poplar and that her religion was Roman Catholic. According to the entry she was 35-years-old, and she had been admitted from Mill Lane. A handwritten comment on the line below these entries states 'pesters Mill Lane, no friends.'

It's not known the exact date that Catherine and Thomas separated, but we know they were still together at the time of the 1881 census as they were recorded as together at 71 George Street, Chelsea South St Jude. Thomas gave his occupation as 'hawker' and Catherine a charwoman. Thomas and George are also there, aged 13 and 7 respectively, and are both recorded as being scholars. There is no mention of Catherine Ann or Frederick, although workhouse records from 1869 have Catherine Ann using them on a couple of occasions at the age of 16. The Fulham Road Workhouse has her recorded as being a machine reeler.

After the separation Thomas moved away with his sons, and used the name Thomas Quinn to draw his army pension so that Catherine couldn't trace them.

Sometime after the separation Catherine moved into 55 Flower and Dean Street, Cooney's Common Lodging House, and met John Kelly, an Irish-born market porter. They would be a couple for the remainder of her life.

Daughter Annie married Louis Phillips on 3rd August 1885. The marriage was performed at the Parish of St Mary Magdalene in Southwark, and they were living at 14 Townsend Street (or Townsend Place, as both are written on the marriage certificate). In 1886 she became bedridden due to her confinement. This was probably when she was pregnant with her son William Frederick Phillips, who was born on 10th August 1886. By this time they were living at King Street in Bermondsey, and had paid her mother to look after her; some time shortly after Annie and her husband moved from Bermondsey, but never gave Catherine their new address in order to stop her visiting and asking for money. She never saw her mother again.

On 14th June 1887 Catherine was admitted to the infirmary under the name Kate Conway. The number on the Whitechapel Infirmary records has Catherine's admittance was 2298. The record also noted that Kate Conway was admitted from 55 Flower and Dean Street, and was 45-years-old. Her calling was given as a hawker, and her status was the wife of Thomas. Her religion was recorded as Roman Catholic, and the reason for admission was due to a burn on her foot. She was admitted at 5.15pm and sent to Ward E.2. After six days Catherine was discharged.

In September 1888 Catherine and John Kelly went hop picking in Kent. Hop picking was a huge annual event that a lot of Londoners would travel to Kent to do in order to make some money. Between four and six weeks from September onwards they would travel, a lot of the time walking the distance to have a holiday picking hops. People would get paid for this, while at the same time getting away from the smog and grime of London life.

That September Catherine and John either didn't earn much money or spent it all, as they returned to the capital on foot, and spent their first night back in London at the casual ward in Shoe Lane where it was reported by newspapers at the time that Catherine had told the Superintendent she believed she knew who Jack the Ripper was and she was going to claim the reward. It was said that she was warned about Jack finding out and killing her also, but she had apparently replied that there was no fear of that.

People who went to a casual ward would do so if they had no other place to stay. They would queue from late afternoon for admission. There were a limited number of beds available, so it was first-come first-served. People would be stripped and bathed, and given some clothing while their own was laundered. They were also given a supper consisting of bread and a pint of gruel. For this they would have to undertake work the next day. For the women this would include picking oakum and laundry duties or cleaning, and for men it would include breaking stones and picking oakum.

On Saturday 29th September, at 8.00am, Catherine met John Kelly at Cooney's and told him there had been trouble at the casual ward and everyone had been turned out early. They agreed that Catherine would go and pawn John's boots as they had no money. They got 2s 6d for them and bought tea, coffee, sugar and food with the money.

Between 10.00am and 11.00am Frederick Wilkinson, deputy of Cooney's, saw Catherine and Kelly eating some breakfast in the kitchen. That afternoon they were in Houndsditch, broke. Catherine said she would try to obtain some money from her daughter Annie in Bermondsey. As they parted ways, she promised to be back by 4.00pm.

At 8.30 that evening Catherine was found outside 29 Aldgate High Street by PC Louis Robinson, after he had noticed a small crowd gathered outside the property. When he tried to prop her up against the wall she was too drunk to stand upright unaided, and fell back down. She was then taken to Bishopsgate Police Station. When asked her name, Catherine replied "Nothing." Station Sergeant James Byfield placed her in a cell to sober up.

At 8.50pm PC Robinson looked in on her and saw that she was asleep. At the inquest he recalled that she smelled very much of alcohol when he found her in Aldgate.

Around 9.00pm, back at Cooney's, John Kelly had heard of Catherine's arrest and told Deputy Wilkinson about it as he paid for a single bed for the night.

By 12.15am Catherine had woken up and was singing softly to herself in her cell. Fifteen minutes later, at 12:30, she asked PC George Hutt when she would be released. He told her she would be released when she could take care of herself. She replied that she was capable of doing that now.

At 12.55am PC Hutt considered Catherine sober enough and released her from her cell, but Sergeant Byfield wouldn't release her without recording a name, so she finally gave her name as 'Mary Ann Kelly' and her address as 6 Fashion Street. Catherine asked PC Hutt what time it was, and on hearing that it was nearly one o'clock exclaimed "I shall get a damned fine hiding when I get home." PC Hutt told her it would serve her right.

At 1.00am, around the same time that Liz Stride's body was discovered in Dutfield's Yard, Catherine Eddowes was released from Bishopsgate Police Station. On her way out PC Hutt asked her to pull the outer door to. As she did so, she said "All right, Goodnight old cock." Exiting the station she turned left heading towards Houndsditch, instead of right in the direction of her lodgings.

At 1.30am PC Edward Watkins was doing his rounds and entered Mitre Square, where he saw nothing. Four minutes later, three men left the Imperial Club at 16-17 Duke Street, Aldgate. These men were Joseph Lawende, Joseph Hyam Levy and Harry Harris. As they were passing the entrance to Church Passage, which led from Duke Street into Mitre Square, they saw a woman with a man about fifteen feet away. The men continued along Duke Street towards Aldgate, leaving the man and woman talking. This woman would later be identified by Lawende as Catherine Eddowes by her clothing.

Approximately six minutes later, PC James Harvey walked along Duke Street and into Church Passage as part of his beat. He didn't look into the square, and later stated that he neither saw nor heard anything.

At 1.45am, five minutes after PC Harvey had walked down Church Passage, PC Watkins again entered Mitre Square and discovered the body of Catherine Eddowes. Her face had been mutilated almost beyond recognition, and a portion of her ear had been sliced off. Watkins ran to the nearby Kearley and Tonge warehouse, where he called for assistance. George Morris, the watchman and a retired officer from the Metropolitan Police, came to his aid. While Watkins stayed with the body Morris ran up Mitre Street blowing his whistle in order to garner attention. PC Harvey heard, then saw Morris running. He went over to him and Morris told him about the dead body. At this time PC Holland was also passing by on his own beat and Morris shouted him over, explaining the discovery. All three returned to Mitre Square, and at 1.50am PC Holland was sent to fetch Dr George Sequeira from his surgery at 34 Jewry Street.

While at Bishopsgate Police Station Inspector Edward Collard was informed at 1.55am that a body had been found in Mitre Square. He sent a constable to notify Dr Frederick Gordon Brown, City Police Surgeon at 17 Finsbury Circus.

Dr Sequeira arrived at Mitre Square at 2.00am and quickly pronounced the victim dead. Shortly afterwards DC Halse, DS Outram, DC Marriott and Inspector Collard all arrived on the scene. Inspector Collard immediately ordered a search of the area. At five minutes past two DC Halse, in the process of searching the area, walked down Middlesex Street and onto Wentworth Street. He saw two men, who gave a reasonable account of themselves. Walking along Goulston Street at about 2.20, he saw nothing suspicious and returned to Mitre Square.

Dr Brown arrived at the scene and undertook an initial examination of Catherine's body:

> *The body was on its back, the head turned towards the left shoulder, and the arms were by the side of the body, as if they had fallen there. Both palms were upwards and the fingers were slightly bent. A thimble was lying on the ground near the right hand. The clothes were drawn up, the left leg was extended straight down, in a line with the body, and the right leg was bent at the thigh and knee There was great disfigurement of the face. The throat was cut across, and below the cut was a neckerchief. The upper part of the dress had been pulled open a little way. The abdomen was all exposed; the intestines were drawn out to a large extent and placed over the right shoulder; a piece of the intestines were quite detached from the body and placed between the left arm and the body.*

At 2.35am Catherine's body was placed in a hand-wheeled ambulance and taken to Golden Lane Mortuary, where the body was stripped and a piece of her ear dropped from her clothing. Inspector Collard, accompanied by DC Halse, made a list and description of the clothing and possessions Catherine had carried about with her. These included a black straw bonnet trimmed with green and black velvet, black beads and black strings. The bonnet was loosely tied, and had partly fallen from the back of her head. There was no blood on the front of the bonnet, even though the back was lying in a pool of blood, which had run from the

neck. A black cloth jacket, with imitation fur edging around the collar and sleeves, had no blood on its front, but a large quantity of blood was discovered on the back, both inside and out.

It was recorded that Catherine was wearing a chintz skirt with three flounces which had a brown button on its waistband. A jagged cut measuring six-and-a-half inches long was found along the waistband. Her brown linsey dress bodice with a black velvet collar had blood on the inside, and the back of its neck and shoulders had a clean cut five inches long. A grey petticoat with a white waistband had a cut one-and-a-half inches long on the front. She was wearing a very old green alpaca skirt with a jagged cut ten-and-a-half inches long in the front of the waistband going downwards. It was bloodstained on the inside and front undercut.

A very old ragged blue skirt with a red flounce, light twill lining had a jagged cut ten-and-a-half inches long going downwards through the waistband; a white calico chemise and a man's white vest with buttons to match down its front with two outside pockets was torn at the back.

All of these items of clothing were bloodstained.

Catherine hadn't been wearing any drawers or stays. She had on a pair of men's lace-up boots with mohair laces, and the right boot had been repaired with red thread.

The belongings she had on her at the time of her death included a piece of red silk gauze with various cuts; one large bloodstained white handkerchief; one bloodstained blue striped bed-ticking pocket with waistband and strings, all three pockets cut through; one white cotton pocket handkerchief with a red and white birds-eye border; one pair of brown ribbed stockings, the feet of which had been repaired with white cotton; twelve pieces of white rag, some slightly bloodstained; two short clay pipes; one tin containing tea, and another containing sugar; one piece of flannel and six pieces of soap, a small tooth comb, one white-handled table knife and one metal teaspoon, a red leather cigarette case with metal fittings, an empty tin match box, a piece of red flannel containing pins and needles, a ball of hemp and a piece of old white apron.

Beside the body, Sergeant Jones of the City of London Police had found three buttons, a thimble and a mustard tin containing two pawn tickets in the name of 'Birrell'.

DC Halse noted there was a section missing from her apron, seemingly cut off.

At 2.55am Metropolitan PC Alfred Long was on his beat along Goulston Street. As he approached the entrance to 108-119 Wentworth Model Dwellings he saw a bloodstained piece of material on the floor – it later proved to be the missing portion of Catherine's apron. Above, he noticed that some writing had been chalked on the black fascia edging of the open doorway. PC Long searched the staircases and landings of the building but found nothing else.

At 5.30am Sir Charles Warren, Commissioner of the Metropolitan Police ordered the graffiti was to be erased. A few officers argued against it being removed, but Warren claimed that leaving it would incite racial tensions in an already volatile atmosphere. He decided against covering it with material until a photographer could arrive, as he felt that could easily have been ripped away. Two policemen had the forethought

SIR C. WARREN VIEWING HANDWRITING ON WALL

to write the wording down in their notebooks, although sadly these versions weren't identical. PC Long wrote "The Juwes are the men that will not be blamed for nothing", while DC Halse noted that it was "The Juwes are not the men that will be blamed for nothing."

The post mortem was performed by the City of London Police Surgeon

CATHERINE EDDOWES

Dr Frederick Brown, and was conducted at 2.30pm on the Sunday
afternoon:

*The temperature of the room was 55 deg. Rigor mortis was well
marked. After careful washing of the left hand a recent bruise, the
size of a sixpence, was discovered on the back of the hand between
the thumb and the first finger. There were a few small bruises on
the right shin of older date. The hands and arms were bronzed as
if from sunburning. There were no bruises on the scalp, back of the
body, or elbows. The witness then described in detail the cuts on the
face, which, he stated, was very much mutilated. The throat was cut
across to the extent of about 6in. or 7in. The sternocleidomastoid
muscle was divided; the cricoid cartilage below the vocal cord was
severed through the middle; the large vessels on the left side of the
neck were severed to the bone, the knife marking the intervertebral
cartilage. The sheath of vessels on the right side was just open; the
carotid artery had a pinhole opening; the internal jugular vein was
open to the extent of an inch and a half – not divided. All the injuries
were caused by some very sharp instrument, like a knife, and pointed.
The cause of death was haemorrhage from the left common carotid
artery. The death was immediate. The mutilations were inflicted
after death. They examined the injuries to the abdomen. The walls
of the abdomen were laid open, from the breast downwards. The cut
commenced opposite the ensiform cartilage, in the centre of the body.
The incision went upwards, not penetrating the skin that was over
the sternum; it then divided the ensiform cartilage, and being gristle
they could tell how the knife had made the cut. It was held so that the
point was towards the left side and the handle towards the right. The
cut was made obliquely. The liver was stabbed as if by the point of a
sharp knife. There was another incision in the liver, and about 2½in.,
and below, the left lobe of the liver was slit through by a vertical
cut. Two cuts were shown by a jag of the skin on the left side. The
abdominal walls were divided vertically in the middle line to within
a quarter of an inch of the navel; the cut then took a horizontal course
for 2½. In to the right side; it then divided the navel on the left side
– round it – and made an incision parallel to the former horizontal
incision, leaving the navel on a tongue of skin. Attached to the navel*

was 2½ in. of the lower part of the rectus muscle of the left side of the abdomen. The incision then took an oblique course to the right. There was a stab of about an inch in the left groin, penetrating the skin in superficial fashion. Below that was a cut of 3in., going through all tissues, wounding the peritoneum to about the same extent. There had not been any appreciable bleeding from the vessels.

Dr Brown concluded that cause of death was blood loss from the throat, and that this was the first wound inflicted. He believed at this point Catherine would have been laid on the ground.

John Kelly learned of Catherine's murder by reading about it in the newspaper two days later, realising it was her when the name 'Birrell' was mentioned – it was a woman he and Catherine had befriended while hop picking. He went to Bishopsgate Police Station and was taken to the mortuary, where he identified the body.

The inquest was held by the City Coroner Mr. Samuel Langham at the Golden Lane Mortuary, where after two full days the jury came back with a verdict of 'Wilful murder by some person unknown.'

8.

MARY KELLY

Mary Kelly was the last of the Canonical Five victims, and to this day a lot of her life is still largely unknown. The majority of information we have was given by her friends and former lover Joe Barnett, and even their knowledge was supplied by Mary herself.

According to contemporary newspaper reports, Mary was also known by the names Marie Jeanette Kelly, 'Black Mary', 'Fair Emma' and 'Ginger'.

According to what she told Barnett, she was born around 1863 in Limerick. Her family moved to Wales when she was young, her father John being a foreman at an iron works. Mary married young, aged sixteen, to a man named Davies. His forename has never been discovered, but he was apparently a collier in the mines. Just two years into their marriage he died in a pit explosion, leaving her a widow at the age of just eighteen. Mary claimed she then moved to Cardiff where she stayed in an infirmary for nine months.

By 1884 Mary was living in London, working as a prostitute in a West End brothel. Soon after she travelled to France with a gentleman but returned to London after just a few weeks, complaining that she didn't like it. On her return Mary moved to the East End, a step down from her West End haunts of a few weeks prior. Her first known address was somewhere off George Street, where she lodged with a Mrs Buki. She then moved in with a man named either Morgan Stone or Morganstone, who lived in Pennington Street, close to Stepney Gasworks.

By 1886 she had left Morganstone and was living with a Mrs Carthy in Breezers Hill. She left there to move in with a man named Joseph Fleming, a plasterer living near Bethnal Green. A short while later Mary and Fleming separated, and she found herself at Cooney's Lodging House on Thrawl Street.

On 8th April 1887 Mary met Joseph Barnett in Commercial Street. He was a fish porter at Billingsgate Market. They went for a drink and arranged to meet the following date, when they agreed to live together, initially taking lodgings on St George Street. They subsequently moved to addresses in Little Paternoster Row and then Brick Lane before moving to 13 Miller's Court, Dorset Street some time in the spring of 1888. The landlord was a man named John McCarthy, a chandler who also owned several low-grade properties that he would rent out. His shop at 27 Dorset Street sold candles, oils and groceries.

Besides one photo taken of the exterior of 13 Miller's Court and a number of newspaper sketches, we are reliant on contemporary descriptions of the small room. It was described as being a single room, 10x12ft, partitioned off from the rear of 26 Dorset Street. The room consisted of a bed, two tables, a wash stand and a fireplace.

The room had two mismatched windows, both looking into the court. It's likely that, given the difference in the positions of these windows from the floor, 13 Miller's Court was at one point two different tiny rooms, such as a pantry or lobby that had been knocked into one room. Two panes of windows in the glass nearest the door had been smashed, with newspaper stuffed into the hole. The windows had been broken by Mary while drunk, according to her neighbour Julia Venturney.

Joseph Fleming would at times visit Mary while she was living with Joe Barnett in Miller's Court. In July 1888 Barnett lost his job, and on 30th October Mary and Joe had their final row, the cause being Mary allowing her prostitute friend Maria Harvey to sleep on the floor of the small room. Joe wasn't happy with this and left, moving to Buller's Lodging House at 24-25 New Street, Bishopsgate. Despite their separation Joe continued to visit Mary on an almost daily basis, and gave her money if he could.

On the night of Thursday 8th November, between 7.00pm and 8.00pm, Joe visited Mary and another woman, most likely Lizzie Albrook, was in her room. She was a 20-year-old who also lived in Miller's Court. She later stated that Mary's last words to her were to warn her not to turn out as she had. Maria Harvey had also been there, but she left shortly before 7.00pm. Around eight o'clock both Joe and Lizzie left Mary's room, with Joe returning to Buller's Lodging House.

Between 10.00 and 11.00pm Maurice Lewis, a tailor from Dorset Street, thought he saw Mary drinking in The Horn of Plenty. She was with some other women. At the inquest Lewis also mentioned the name 'Dan'; this was probably Daniel Barnett, Joseph's brother. Joseph was later reported as saying that Daniel had been to see Mary on the night of her murder, so it was more than likely that it was indeed Joe Barnett's brother that Maurice Lewis saw, and not Joe himself. One of the other woman Lewis saw he recognised as a lady named Julia – possibly Julia Venturney, a widowed woman who lived at 1 Miller's Court.

The next sighting of Mary was by Mary Ann Cox, at 11.45pm. Cox was a 31-year-old widow and prostitute who lived at 5 Miller's Court, the last house on the left-hand of the court. Due to the cold weather she had decided to go home to keep warm. As she walked up Dorset Street she recognised Mary walking ahead of her with a large-built man. The couple went up the court a few steps ahead of her. Cox described the man as being in his mid-30s, about 5ft 5in tall with a blotchy face, a carroty moustache and small side whiskers. The man was carrying a quart of beer, and Cox believed they were both drunk. She followed behind them into Miller's Court and greeted Mary as she passed Mary's door. Mary mumbled a reply, and although she was very drunk and could barely answer she did manage to reply 'Goodnight.'

Just a few minutes later Mary Ann Cox heard Mary singing the popular music hall ballad *A Violet From Mother's Grave*. About fifteen minutes later, Cox returned to Dorset Street, and as she again passed Mary's room she could still hear her neighbour singing the same song.

It would have been around this time that Mary would have eaten her last meal of fish and potatoes.

At approximately 12.30am Catherine Pickett, one of Mary's neighbours on the floor above, had by now had enough of Mary's singing and was about to go and knock on her door to complain but she was stopped by her husband, who told her to 'Leave that poor woman alone.'

Around 1.00am Cox returned to her room and as she passed No. 13 she heard Mary still singing; light could be seen from behind the make-shift curtains. Elizabeth Prater, another woman who lived above Mary at 20 Miller's Court, returned to her room at about 1.30am. She had just spent around thirty minutes at the entrance to Miller's Court waiting to meet the man she lived with, who didn't show up. She heard no noise from Mary's room, but could see the light visible through the partition wall when going up the stairs. Prater placed two chairs against her door as a means of security and then got into bed without getting undressed.

By 2.00am George Hutchinson had just reached Commercial Street, having apparently walked back from Romford. He was a resident at the Victoria Working Men's Home but was unable to get his bed as he had arrived too late. On reaching the corner of Thrawl Street Hutchinson passed a man but paid no attention to him.

At the corner of Commercial Street and Flower and Dean Street he met Mary Kelly, who had evidently gone back out. Hutchinson knew Mary well and she asked him for a loan of sixpence, but he replied he was unable to do so as he had spent all his money at Romford. Mary then started walking in the direction Hutchinson had just come from, leaving him with the parting words 'Good morning, I must go and find some money.' The man Hutchinson had passed at Thrawl Street was walking towards them, and as Hutchinson walked away the stranger approached Mary and, putting his hand on her shoulder, said something to her which she replied to with a laugh and the words 'All right', to which the man replied 'You will be alright for what I have told you.' They walked off together up Commercial Street, in the direction of Dorset Street.

George Hutchinson had by this time reached The Queen's Head on the junction of Fashion Street. He was stood under a lamp post as the couple

approached, and Hutchinson got a good look at the man as they passed, although the man tried to duck his head away from view.

Hutchinson decided to follow the couple and they stopped at Miller's Court, where he heard Mary tell the man 'All right, my dear, come along, you will be comfortable.' The man put his arm around Kelly and she kissed him, then said that she had lost her handkerchief. At this the man handed her a red one and they both walked towards her room.

Hutchinson spent the next hour standing by a lamp next to the Crossingham's Lodging House, opposite the arched entrance to Miller's Court.

The description of the man he later gave in his police statement was so detailed that a lot of people have questioned the validity of it. He said that the man was aged about 35 or 36, 5ft 6in tall, with a pale complexion, dark hair, dark eyes and eyelashes. He also had a slight moustache, curled up at each end. He was 'very surly looking', and dressed in a long dark coat, its collar and cuffs trimmed with Astrakhan, and a dark jacket over a light waistcoat, dark trousers and a dark felt hat turned down in the middle. He was wearing button boots and gaiters with white buttons. He wore a very thick gold chain, white linen collar, a black tie with horse shoe pin. All in all, a respectable appearance. He walked very 'sharp', and had a Jewish appearance. Hutchinson believed he would be able to identify him if he saw him again.

For some reason George Hutchinson didn't make this statement until a few days after the murder, going to the police on the day of the inquest, so he was never called to give an account and the only records we have are his police statement and newspaper reports, which seem even more embellished than the statement.

Hutchinson stood opposite Miller's Court until 3.00am when, on hearing the church bells ring in the hour, he decided he was wasting his time and moved on to find somewhere else to sleep. Around this time Mary Ann Cox returned home for the last time. This time, as she passed Mary's room there was no sound nor any light.

At 4.00am Elizabeth Prater, who had been asleep in the room above Mary's, was awoken by her kitten walking across her on the bed. At that time she heard a faint cry of 'Oh, murder.'

Sarah Lewis, visiting friends at 2 Miller's Court after having an argument with her husband, also heard a cry at this time. However, as it was an apparently common shout at this time it's not sure if it was connected to Mary Kelly's murder in any way. Sarah Lewis did see a man loitering around the court between 2.00 and 3.00am, and it's possible that this was George Hutchinson.

Caroline Maxwell, the wife of Henry Maxwell, a lodging house deputy at 14 Dorset Street, claimed that she saw Mary Kelly at 8.30 the following morning, being sick outside Miller's Court. This statement has not been taken seriously by most people, as it seems unlikely that Mary would still be alive at this point.

At 10.45am Thomas Bowyer was sent by John McCarthy to collect the rent arrears which Mary owed him. At this time she owed 29s, a huge amount – a total of six weeks' rent. Bowyer entered the court and on reaching number thirteen knocked, but received no answer. He pulled back the curtain covering the smaller window and saw the mutilated remains of a body. He hurried to find John McCarthy, who returned with him, and on seeing for himself the gruesome sight sent Bowyer to Commercial Street Police Station.

The inquest into Mary Kelly's death was opened on 12th November 1888 by Dr Roderick Macdonald MP, the coroner for North-Eastern District. Dr George Bagster Phillips, who had attended the scene, gave his testimony to describe what he had seen at 13 Miller's Court:

The mutilated remains of a female were lying two thirds over towards the edge of the bedstead nearest the door. She had only her chemise on, or some undergarment. I am sure that the body had been removed subsequent to the injury which caused her death from that side of the bedstead that was nearest the wooden partition, because of the larger quantity of blood under the bedstead and the saturated condition of the sheet and the palliasse at the corner nearest the partition. The blood was produced by the severance of the carotid artery, which was the cause of death. The injury was inflicted while the deceased was lying on the right side of the bed.

The inquest evidence gave an insight to the horrors that were inflicted on Mary Jane Kelly. Dr Thomas Bond's post mortem report reveals how badly she was mutilated:

The body was lying naked in the middle of the bed, the shoulders flat, but the axis of the body inclined to the left side of the bed. The head was turned on the cheek. The left arm was close to the body, with the forearm flexed at a right angle and lying across the abdomen, the right arm was slightly abducted from the body and rested on the mattress, the elbow bent, the forearm supine with fingers clenched. The legs were wide apart, the left thigh at right angles to the trunk and the right forming an obtuse angle with the pubes.

The whole surface of the abdomen and thighs was removed and the abdominal cavity emptied of its viscera. The breasts were cut off, the arms mutilated by several jagged wounds and the face hacked beyond recognition of the features. The tissues of the neck were severed all round down to the bone.

The viscera were found in various parts viz; the uterus and kidneys with one breast under the head, the other breast by the right foot, the liver between the feet, the intestines by the right side and the spleen by the left side of the body.

The flaps removed from the abdomen and thighs were on a table.

The bed clothing at the right corner was saturated with blood, and on the floor beneath was a pool of blood covering about 2 square feet. The wall by the right side of the bed and in a line with the neck marked by blood which had struck it in a number of separate splashes.

The face was gashed in all directions, the nose, cheeks, eyebrows, and ears being partly removed. The lips were blanched and cut by several incision running obliquely down to the chin. There were also numerous cuts extending irregularly across all the features. The neck was cut through the skin and other tissue right down to the vertebrae, the 5th and 6th being deeply notched. The skin cuts in the front of the neck showed distinct ecchymosis.

The air passage was cut at the lower part of the larynx through the cricoid cartilage.

Both breasts were more or less removed by circular incisions, the muscle down to the ribs being attached to the breasts. The intercostals between the 4th, 5th and 6th ribs were cut through and the contents of the thorax visible through the openings. The skin and tissues of the abdomen from the costal arch to the pubes were removed in 3 large flaps. The right thigh was denuded in front to the bone, the flaps of skin, including the external organs of generation, and part of the right buttock. The left thigh was stripped of skin, fascia and muscles as far as the knee.

The left calf showed a long gash through skin and tissues to the deep muscles and reaching from the knee to 5 inches above the ankle. Both arms and forearms had extensive jagged wounds. The thumb showed a small superficial incision about 1 inch long; with extravasation of blood in the skin and there were several abrasions on the back of the hand moreover showing the same condition. On opening the thorax it was found that the right lung was minimally adherent by old firm adhesions. The lower part of the lung was broken and torn away.

The left lung was intact; it was adherent at the apex and there were a few adhesions over the side. In the substance of the lung there were several nodules of consolidation.

The pericardium was open below and the heart was absent.

In the abdominal cavity there was some partly digested food of fish and potatoes, and similar food was found in the remains of the stomach attached to the intestines.

The inquest verdict was unsurprising: 'Wilful murder against some person or persons unknown.'

9.

CANONICAL FIVE?

Martha Tabram was discovered lying on her back on 7th August 1888 by John Reeves as he descended the stairs on his way to work at around 4.55am. She had been repeatedly stabbed, a total of 39 times. Her hands were lying by her side and her clothes were in disarray, her dress torn open.

Ever since the murders were committed there have been questions as to whether Martha was indeed a victim of Jack the Ripper, and certain police officials at the time including Frederick Abberline, Sir Robert Anderson, Inspector Reid and Walter Dew believed that she was.

In a thought-provoking dissertation found on Casebook.org titled 'The Case for Re-Canonizing Martha Tabram', Quentin L Pittman makes some very interesting points. The observations he raised strengthens the authors' argument that Martha Tabram should in fact be considered a Jack the Ripper victim.

Pittman mentions the similarity of the position of Tabram's body to that of Nichols, Chapman and Eddowes: 'All four women were found lying on their backs, clothes disarranged. The upper part of Tabram's and Eddowes' dress was torn open and their fingers bent. Aside from Nichols, the women's lower clothing was thrown up as well. While the parallels may seem slight, they are an important beginning in establishing a consistent likeness between the attacks on these women.'

It is generally believed that as Tabram's throat wasn't cut, or the fact that she wasn't dismembered or mutilated, meant that her killer couldn't have been Jack the Ripper; a closer examination shows that this may not be the case. Admittedly Tabram's throat wasn't cut, but nine of the stab wounds to her body were aimed at her throat. Her breasts, stomach and vaginal area were also targeted, which were the same areas where the knife wounds that were inflicted also Nichols, Chapman, Eddowes and Kelly.

Another contentious point was that Dr Killeen believed Martha's killer to be right-handed, whereas the killer of the other victims was initially believed to be left-handed; this would suggest two separate killers. However, this view seems to have changed and by the murder of Mary Kelly most people believed Jack the Ripper to actually be right-handed.

It is also worth pointing out that, like the other victims, Martha was local to the area, a prostitute, was murdered on a weekend, and had very similar features to Polly, Annie and Catherine. All were mutilated after death.

While it is agreed there is one big difference in that the immediate cause of Martha's death wasn't her throat being cut, she did in fact suffer multiple knife wounds to that area. This difference could be easily explained in that the killer was refining his method. It is known that a murderer will hone his skills as he gains more confidence.

Liz Stride is included in the Canonical Five: she was murdered on the same night as Catherine Eddowes, and her throat had been cut. While it is without a doubt she died in the same fashion as other Jack the Ripper victims, this method of killing which was not unique to the Ripper – there were many other killers in London!

We can never really know if Liz was working as a prostitute or not that night. While it's likely the IMWEC would frown upon solicitation on their grounds, if prostitutes had wanted to use the yard it would have been easy to see that trade would have been readily accessible given the amount of men who frequented the club.

A perfect example of how prostitutes and customers – and murderers

– could easily evade detection is given in an article that appeared in the *Pall Mall Gazette* of 2nd October 1890:

> *When you push open the gate it is as dark as Erebus; when the gate is pushed back there is an effectual screen from any prying passer-by, although passers-by, who are constituted very largely of the foreigners who reside in the locality, are far too scared to ever peep inside that gate with its terrible history; and, finally, there is always singing or some other form of entertainment going on at the International Club next door to effectually drown a faint shriek. But what about the policeman on the beat you say? The police on that beat have got so tired of opening that gate and finding nothing there since the murder that they have long ago despaired of ever finding anything and consequently pass it now with the most complete indifference. And even should by the most remote possibility, the murderer be disturbed by anybody opening the gate from the street entrance, he is by no means caught in a trap, for there are plenty of back yards that can be scaled, and a great many courts and passages, leading to Berner Street and other streets to be easily reached.*

The more relevant aspect in this case is the time and location of the murder. Liz was attacked much earlier in the night than the other victims, in a populated area that was brightly lit or at least lit enough for Israel Schwartz to be able to describe her and her assault; nothing like any of the other murders. The fact that the attack was witnessed by Schwartz and 'pipe man' shows a different modus operandi to the killer in other cases. The attack itself seemed more 'personal' than random. The man was seen talking to Liz, and then trying to drag her out onto the street before pushing her to the floor. Liz then screamed softly three times.

In our opinion this is not the reaction of a woman who had just been accosted by a stranger. Surely a physically-able woman, when being attacked by some person not known to her and thrown to the ground, would yell and scream as loud as she possibly could? Liz showed nothing of the fear one would expect of a prostitute in that area of London after three high profile murders.

Ever since the murder was committed it has been questioned as to whether Liz was indeed a Jack the Ripper victim. It is our opinion that she was not.

10

OTHER VICTIMS?

In addition to the more well-known victims, those widely recognised as the victims of Jack the Ripper, several women were murdered before and in the years following the so-called Autumn of Terror in the Whitechapel area in circumstances that mirrored aspects of the more infamous murders.

Emma Smith

Emma Elizabeth Smith died in April 1888, four months before the murder of Martha Tabram. Even now, after years of searching, researchers have yet to find a verified family tree for Emma. What is known is that she was born around 1843. Some newspaper accounts of her murder state that by 1888 she was a widow, but according to the Hospital Administration Register she was recorded as married and working as a charwoman. A plausible candidate going on the scant information we have on her is that of Emma Elizabeth Smith living in the Whitechapel area in the 1881 census with her husband John Smith.

They were living at 118 Central Street, St Luke. John was 45-years-old and had been born in Kent. In the census he was classed as a pensioner retired from the army, the 35th Regiment. Emma was 37-years-old and had been born in Plymouth. A search through the records brings up a possible match to John Smith, born 1843 and who married Emma Elizabeth Wells (born 1844) at St Mary's in Portsea, Hampshire. We have Emma Smith born in Plymouth, Devon, living at Northumbria Barracks with her son Thomas Smith aged 9, who was born in Portsmouth.

Emma had reportedly been a prostitute for a number of years, when on 2nd April 1888 she left her lodgings at 18 George Street, Spitalfields at about 7.00pm. Not a lot is known about the events that occurred that night, but between 4.00am and 5.00am she returned to her lodgings with injuries to her head and face. Her ear was nearly torn completely off, and she held her shawl between her legs to staunch the blood that was flowing from internal wounds from where a blunt object had been forced into her vagina, ripping through her perineum. She was helped to the London Hospital, where she died the following day from peritonitis as a result of her injuries.

An inquest was held on 7th April 1888 at the London Hospital by Mr Wynne Baxter. First to give testimony was the Deputy Keeper of 18 George Street, Mrs Mary Russell, who explained how Emma had managed to tell her on arriving back at the lodging house despite her terrible injuries that she had been attacked by three men whilst on her way home. She couldn't describe them, except to say that one was around nineteen years old. Emma complained of pains in her lower body and Mary Russell had helped her to the hospital. On the way, while they were walking past Osborn Street, Emma managed to point out the place where the attack had taken place.

The next person to give testimony was George Haslip, House Surgeon at the London Hospital. He described how Emma had been admitted on the early morning of 3rd April. He believed that although the deceased had been drinking, she wasn't intoxicated. He declined to go into detail on the specific injuries that Emma had received, but explained that the victim had "been bleeding from head and ear and other injuries of a revolting nature."

He related to the Coroner how Emma had managed to tell him of the events leading up to the attack. At about 1.30am, while passing Whitechapel Church, she noticed some men coming towards her. She

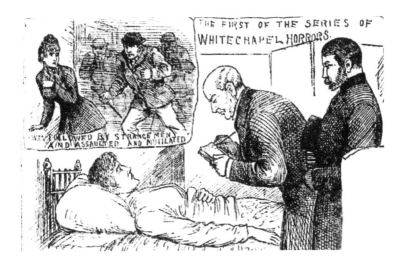

THE FIRST OF THE SERIES OF WHITECHAPEL HORRORS.

crossed the road to avoid them, but they followed her and robbed and attacked her, causing the injuries described. Haslip believed the injuries sustained through the assault with the blunt object had the peritonitis which was the cause of her death.

The police officer in attendance at the inquest was Chief Inspector West of H Division, who stated he knew nothing of the case other than what he had read in the newspapers. He had questioned the constables on the beat in the area, and they reported they knew nothing.

The inquest was closed with the verdict "Murder by some person or persons unknown."

Rose Mylett

Others put forward as being possible victims of Jack the Ripper were all murdered after Mary Kelly. The first of these was Rose Mylett, who was also reported as using the names Catherine Millet, 'Drunken' Lizzie Davis and 'Fair' Alice Downey.

Rose, as she was known to her friends, was born Catherine Mylett on 8th December 1859. According to her mother she married an upholsterer known as Davis and they had a daughter, Florence, born on

12th September 1880 in Mile End Old Town.

In 1881 'Rose' was living at 40 Lincoln Street using the name Kate Davis. It's probable that she had already separated from her husband; she could have been widowed, but the 1881 census has her as 'married.' She was classed as the 'Head' of the household. Six-month-old Florence was living with her.

Very little is known of Rose's whereabouts over the next few years, but it is known that Florence was in and out of workhouses up until at least the age of fourteen.

On 20th January 1888 Florence was admitted to Bromley House in Stepney, which was also known as the Stepney Union Workhouse found on St Leonard Street in Bromley. There is limited information available on the workhouse record, but it does say that Florence was born in 1882 and that she was the child of Rose Mylett alias Davis. Florence was discharged to 'Sutton' on 24th January 1888, as were most of the children on the page indicating it was likely a school or workhouse for the children of paupers or orphaned children.

Interestingly enough, scrolling down to the bottom of the page there is a record of a Rose Mylett, alias Davis, also admitted here on 9th March 1888. She was born in 1862 and noted as a farm worker. She was classed as single, and on 14th March she was released from 'sa OR.' This is likely shorthand for 'from sick asylum on own request'.

A few days later Florence was admitted to Brighton Road School in the South Metropolitan School District. In the 'Nearest known relation' column it simply states 'Mother in sick asylum.' On 20th March 1888 Florence was admitted again to Bromley House. She was discharged on 24th March: 'PH to Sutton.' Florence seemed to spend a lot of her childhood years in and out of school workhouses after Rose's death.

On 26th February 1889 at Bromley House it's recorded that Florence Mylett (alias Davis), born 1882, an orphan of no occupation was admitted. She was discharged on 28th February from Sutton at her own request to Mile End.

On 29th September 1890 the Banstead Road School, Kensington and Chelsea admissions note Florence Mylett, born 1880, in attendance. The date of admittance was 19th September 1890, and the name of her last school was Mile End Old Town. The date of her discharge was recorded as 17th January 1894.

The 1891 census recorded Florence at the Surrey Ewell District School and Cottage Homes. She was classed as a scholar, a child aged 10. She was born in London, Mile End.

On 18th January 1894, just one day after her discharge from the Banstead Road School in Kensington, Florence was admitted to the Stepney workhouse, by 'order of board'.

The final record, dated 1st March 1894 is a discharge record for back to the Bancroft school.

It's not known whether Rose was living in Sutton at this time or if she had a house there; it would seem unlikely, as the next documented sighting of her is on 19th December 1888 in the East End.

At 7.55 that evening she was seen by Charles Ptolomey, a night attendant of an infirmary. He said he saw her in Poplar High Street, speaking to two sailors. He heard her saying "No, no, no!" to one of the sailors, and although he felt it was enough to warrant attention he didn't actually do anything. He felt she appeared to be sober.

The next known sighting was at 2.30am, when Alice Graves spotted Rose outside The George public house in Commercial Road with two men. Graves later said that Rose appeared drunk.

Rose was discovered at 4.15am by Police Sergeant Robert Golding, when he came across her lifeless body while patrolling Clark's Yard, between 184 and 186 Poplar High Street.

The post-mortem report given by Dr Brownfield was detailed:

> *Blood was oozing from the nostrils, and there was a slight abrasion on the right side of the face... One [sic] the neck there was a mark which had evidently been caused by a cord drawn tightly round the neck, from the spine to the left ear. Such a mark would be made by a four thread cord. There were also impressions of the thumbs and middle and index fingers of some person plainly visible on each side of the neck. There were no injuries to the arms or legs. The brain was gorged with an almost black fluid blood. The stomach was full*

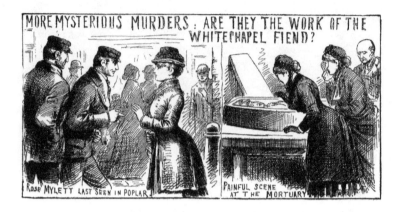

MORE MYSTERIOUS MURDERS : ARE THEY THE WORK OF THE WHITECHAPEL FIEND?

ROSE MYLETT LAST SEEN IN POPLAR.

PAINFUL SCENE AT THE MORTUARY

of meat and potatoes, which had only recently been eaten. Death was due to strangulation. Deceased could not have done it herself. The marks on her neck were probably caused by her trying to pull the cord off. He thought the murderer must have stood at the left rear of the woman, and, having the ends of the cord round his hands, thrown it round her throat, crossed his hands, and thus strangled her. If it had been done this way, it would account for the mark not going completely round the neck.

Assistant Commissioner Dr Robert Anderson didn't agree with these findings. After looking into the case he observed that there was no trace of a struggle on the ground near where her body was found, no torn clothing, no scratches on the body and no second set of footprints anywhere on the soft ground around her. He also believed the body lay 'naturally'. Due to this he requested that Dr Thomas Bond re-examined the body in order to give a second opinion. While waiting on Dr Bond's examination, his personal assistant together with a senior police surgeon examined Mylett, and were both of the opinion that it was wilful murder by strangulation.

Five days after the murder Dr Bond finally examined the body. He couldn't find any signs of strangulation around her neck, and no other evidence commonly associated with strangulation such as a protruding tongue or clenched fists. Dr Bond also believed that it wasn't murder, suspecting that Mylett had in fact fallen over while drunk and had been choked by her stiff collar.

She was lying on her left side and her body was still warm, with no obvious signs of injury. Rose's cause of death created some confusion and later a little animosity between the Police force and the coroner's office, to the point it was said Assistant Commissioner Robert Anderson and the CID refused to invest any further time in the case after the coroner sided with Divisional Surgeon Dr Matthew Brownfield and his assistant Mr Harris, who had been originally at a loss to explain the cause as there were no identifiable wounds or injuries to her body, until they noticed a faint mark resembling what they believed could be the imprint of a piece of string. It was then that strangulation was considered. Anderson had in fact believed that there was no sign of a struggle or that strangulation had occurred; he believed that Rose had tripped on the hem of her dress and strangled herself with her starched dress collar.

The inquest was opened at Poplar Town Hall on 21st December 1888, then postponed until 2nd January 1889 and again until 9th January. It was presided over by Coroner Wynne Baxter. Given that there were two differing opinions as to whether it was murder or a natural death, Baxter sided strongly with Dr Brownfield's opinion that Rose had been murdered, rather than that of the police who, as they hadn't found any discarded string or other suitable ligature material discarded near Mylett's body, agreed with Dr Bond's opinion that death was either accidental or from natural causes.

In his summing up of the evidence, Baxter stated:

> *After Dr. Brownfield and his assistant, duly qualified men, came to the conclusion that this was a case of homicidal strangulation, someone had a suspicion that the evidence was not satisfactory. At all events, you've heard that doctor after doctor went down to view the body without my knowledge or sanction as coroner. I did not wish to make that a personal matter, but I had never received such treatment before. Of the five doctors who saw the body, Dr. Bond was the only one who considered the case was not one of murder. Dr. Bond did not*

see the body until five days after her death and he was, therefore, at a disadvantage. Dr. Bond stated that if this was a case of strangulation he should have expected to find the skin broken, but it was clearly shown, on reference being made to the records of the Indian doctors in the cases of Thug murders, that there were no marks whatever left. Other eminent authorities agreed with that view.

The jury agreed with the coroner and brought back a verdict of "Wilful murder by person or persons unknown."

Alice McKenzie

Not a lot is known about Alice's early life, but according to John McCormack, the man she was living with at the time of her murder, she was born about 1849 in Peterborough, making her around forty years old at the time of her death. He stated she was a hardworking woman, washing and cleaning for local Jews. He didn't know if she had any children. Reportedly also known as 'Clay Pipe' Alice and Alice Bryant, she was known as a prostitute to the police, and she got her 'Clay Pipe' nickname due to her fondness of having multiple clay pipes on her person at all times.

On 15th July 1891, at 7.00pm, Alice returned to the room she shared with John McCormack at Tenpenny's Lodging House at 52 Gun Street. They had been lodging there for about four months at that time, but had stayed at Tenpenny's on and off for twelve months in total. Alice told McCormack that she was going to go straight to bed as she had been working all day. McCormack replied that he didn't believe her, as he had been told by others that she hadn't worked at all that day.

Just before 6.00am the following morning McKenzie was seen getting breakfast for McCormack before he went to work. After he had departed she spent most of the day in the lodging house kitchen smoking her clay pipes. According to the deputy housekeeper, at one point she was also drinking. Alice went to meet McCormack from work after 3.00pm and they returned to the lodging house around 4.00pm. McCormack, who had himself been drinking, went straight to bed after giving Alice 1s 8d – 8d to pay for their lodgings, and the rest for her to spend how she wanted. Alice went downstairs but didn't pay the rent, instead leaving the lodging house. She was next seen in Little Paternoster Row talking to Caroline Slade, sister of the deputy housekeeper of Tenpenny's lodging house, Elizabeth Ryder.

Caroline felt that Alice had been drinking. Alice returned to the lodging house by 4.45pm, where she was seen by fellow lodger Isabella Hayes. She seemed in good spirits and was smoking a pipe in the kitchen. Hayes later said that she saw Alice leave the lodging house at around 6.30pm, adding that it wasn't unusual for Alice to go out for a little drink once McCormack had gone to bed.

The next sighting was at around 7.10pm, when Alice was seen with a young blind boy named George Dixon, who also lodged at Tenpenny's. She had accompanied him to The Royal Cambridge Tavern, a public house near the Royal Cambridge Music Hall. Dixon later stated that he had heard Alice ask someone to stand her a drink, and a man answered he would. A few minutes later Alice took George back to the lodging house. Once there, Alice told the other lodgers that whilst in the pub she had met a man from Tottenham she knew, and that she was going to go back to meet him. She left her clay pipe with fellow lodger Margaret O'Brien until she returned.

Just after 10.30pm John McCormack awoke and went downstairs to be told by the deputy Elizabeth Ryder that Alice had not paid the rent. He asked what he was supposed to do – should he go and walk the streets as well? She replied that he should do nothing of the sort, and to return to his room and go to bed. He did so, as he had to be up for work at 5.30am the following morning.

At 11.40pm Alice was seen walking hurriedly past 27 Brick Lane by three women, Margaret Franklin, Catherine Hughes and Sarah Mahoney. Alice said hello when they called out, but told them she couldn't stop to talk as she hurried down the street in the direction of Whitechapel.

At 12.15am PC Joseph Allen was standing under a street lamp in Castle Alley, just off Whitechapel High Street, while he had a rest and something to eat. He saw nothing untoward, and after standing there for a few minutes he saw another officer enter the alley. This was PC Walter

Andrews. He too remained in the alley for a few minutes, but noticed nothing suspicious.

At 12.45am it began to rain. Five minutes later PC Andrews returned to Castle Alley on his beat and came across the body of a woman lying on the pavement, on the edge of the kerbstone with her feet towards the building and her head lying eastward. Alice's clothes had been pulled up to her chin and her legs and lower body were exposed. PC Andrews saw blood flowing from two injuries to her neck and blood across her abdomen, which was later to have been discovered that it had been mutilated.

The inquest into Alice McKenzie's death commenced on Wednesday, 17th July 1889 and was presided over by Mr Wynne Baxter. It was held at the Working Lads' Institute, on Whitechapel Road. Witnesses to Alice's last movements gave their testimony, and on the second day H Division's Detective Edmund Reid took the stand:

I received a call to Castle Alley about five minutes past 1 on the morning of the murder. I dressed and ran down at once. On arriving at Castle Alley I found the Wentworth Street end blocked by a policeman. On arriving at the back of the baths I saw the deceased woman. I saw she had a cut on the left side of the throat, and there was a quantity of blood under the head which was running into the gutter. The clothes were up and her face was slightly turned towards the road. She was lying on her back. I felt the face and body, and found they were warm. Dr Phillips arrived. At the time I arrived I ascertained the fact that the other end (Whitechapel) was blocked and search was being made through the alley and also in the immediate neighbourhood The deputy-superintendent and his wife at the baths were seen and stated they heard nothing unusual. After the body had been examined by the doctor it was placed on the police ambulance, and underneath the body of the deceased was found the short clay pipe produced. The pipe was broken and there was blood on it, and in the bowl was some unburnt tobacco. I also found a bronze farthing underneath the clothes of the deceased. There was also blood on the farthing. I produce a rough plan of Castle Alley; a correct copy of which will be set by the draughtsman.

After going on to explain how the police had been thorough in their search of the area and the positioning of the lamp there, Reid also noted that he believed no stranger would have gone down to the alley where Alice was found unless taken there. He also commented on how the area was always a busy thoroughfare, and that two police constables were continually passing through the alley at night whilst on their beat. He observed that while it was raining when Alice was discovered, the ground under her body was dry. He gave his opinion that while the alley was poorly lit, he felt the five lamps there were sufficient enough.

Dr George Bagster Phillips, Divisional Surgeon of H Division, was responsible for examining Alice's body in situ and for performing the post-mortem. He explained on the second day of the inquest how he had examined the body on the night of the murder, after which it transported to the 'shed' that was being used as a mortuary in Montague Street, Whitechapel, where he performed the post-mortem. It was the same mortuary where Tabram, Nichols, Chapman and later Frances Coles were taken. He took the opportunity to air his grievances about how inadequate he felt the facilities of the 'mortuary' were, saying it was "a most inconvenient and altogether ill-appointed place for such a purpose. It tended greatly to the thwarting of justice having such a place to perform such an examination in."

He then went on to describe the post-mortem, which was reported in *The Times* of 19th July 1889 as follows:

> *With several colleagues he made the examination about 2 o'clock, when rigor mortis was well marked. The witness then described the wounds, of which there were several, and these were most of them superficial cuts on the lower part of the body. There were several old scars, and there was the loss of the top of the right thumb, apparently caused by some former injury. The wound in the neck was 4in. long, reaching from the back part of the muscle, which were almost entirely divided. It reached to the fore part of the neck to a point 4 in. below the chin. There was a second incision, which must have commenced from behind and immediately below the first. The cause of death was syncope, arising from the loss of blood through the divided carotid vessels, as such death probably was almost instantaneous.*

Dr Phillips was recalled the following day and expanded on his findings, telling the inquest that when one of the mortuary attendants removed the clothes from the deceased he discovered a short clay pipe, which he then threw it to the floor. Phillips told how he had placed the broken pieces on a ledge at the bottom of the post-mortem table, but they had since disappeared. He also explained how he had found five marks on the victim's abdomen, which he believed were caused by the fingernails and thumbnail of a hand.

He felt she hadn't been dead longer than half an hour when he first saw the body. He was emphatic that the injuries to her throat were in no way similar to the previous Whitechapel cases.

The jury returned a verdict of "Wilful murder against some person or persons unknown."

Frances Coles

Frances Coles was born on 17th September 1859 at 18 Crucifix Lane in Bermondsey, to bootmaker James William Coles and Mary Ann Coles, née Carney. Like previous victims, not much is known about Frances's younger years, but by 1880 she was living on her own and had a job at a wholesale chemist's shop putting stoppers in bottles, a job she would tell her elder sister, Mary Ann, was painful on her knuckles. She persevered with it for a few years before finally leaving.

In 1883 she was prostituting around the areas of Whitechapel, Shoreditch and Bow. On 16th December 1890, while having tea with Mary Ann, Frances blatantly lied and claimed she was still working in the chemist and living with an old lady at Richard Street, Commercial Road. However, Mary Ann could see through the story and noticed how Frances looked poor and very dirty. On the last few occasions they met she had smelled alcohol on her breath.

The last time Frances's father saw her was when she visited him on 6th February 1891. She admitted that she was no longer working at the chemist, but did insist she was still living at Richard Street. James later stated that he wasn't aware of his daughter's profession until after her death.

The night before her death Frances met up with a former client by the name of James Sadler. He was a 53-year-old merchant seaman and ship's fireman, who had been discharged from the SS *Fez* the previous day. They spent the night together at Spitalfields Chambers, a common lodging house at 8 White's Row, and also the following day, frequenting pubs in the area.

That night, at around 7.30pm, Sadler gave Frances 2s 6d which she used to buy a new black crepe hat from a millinery shop at 25 Nottingham Street in Bethnal Green. The man who served her, Peter Hawkes, later told police that she was "three sheets to the wind."

Her actions on the night of her murder are well documented. Between 9.00 and 10.00pm Frances and James Sadler had an argument after he was mugged by a woman and two men, but Frances had just stood by and done nothing to aid him.

By 11.30pm a drunken Frances returned to their lodgings at Spitalfields Chambers, where she quickly fell asleep on a bench in the kitchen. Sadler returned shortly afterwards, his face bloodied and bruised, but was told to leave as he had no money to pay for his room. At about 12.30am Frances awoke and was also told to leave, as she too was apparently penniless.

At 1.30am she was at Shuttleworth's Eating House in Wentworth Street, where she sat to eat a meal of mutton and bread. It's not entirely certain how she paid for this; maybe she had turned a trick or she had a little money left from what Sadler had given her earlier in the day.

Frances moved on to Commercial Road, where she accepted the invitation of a man in a cheese cutter hat who had propositioned her, even after she had just witnessed the man try to solicit fellow prostitute Ellen Callana. When Callana refused the man he hit her in the face, giving her a black eye. Amazingly, even after what she had just witnessed and against Callana's warnings, Frances still went off with the man.

At 2.15am PC Ernest Thompson 240H, who was in only his second week as a policeman and on his first night alone, was on his beat walking along Chamber Street when he heard the sound of footsteps running away in the direction of Mansell Street. He turned into Swallow Gardens and shone his lamp into the darkness, where he saw the body of Frances Coles, blood running from her slit throat as she lay on the ground. To his horror he realised she was still alive when she opened and closed one eye. Although there was a possibility that Thompson could have chased after and captured the killer, police procedure dictated that as the victim was alive he had to remain with her.

The probable method of the attack was pieced together by Dr Phillips, who performed the autopsy, and Dr Oxley, who was the first doctor to arrive at the scene. They both believed she had been violently thrown to the ground and her throat cut, but Dr Phillips believed that the assailant had most likely cut the throat from the side, grasping her chin and cutting left to right. He was also of the opinion that her throat had been cut three times: left to right, right to left and back again left to right, and that the killer showed no signs of anatomical knowledge. Dr Oxley, however, believed that Frances's throat had been cut from the front, and that the body had been tilted so that there would have been very little spray of blood on the killer. He was of the opinion that her throat had

only been cut twice, since there was only one incision but two wounds in the larynx. Frances's clothes were in order, and there was none of the abdominal mutilation that was a common feature in the Ripper killings.

Given the argument and bad feeling between Frances Coles and James Sadler when they parted ways earlier in the evening, Sadler quickly became the prime suspect in her murder and even at one point for other Jack the Ripper murders. He was charged with the murder of Frances Coles on 16th February 1891, but acquitted following the inquest and magistrates' hearing four days later.

It was the contention of Chief Constable Melville Macnaghten and a few other police officers that Sadler was guilty despite this verdict, but he could never again be charged with her murder.

Frances Coles' death was recorded as 'Wilful murder by person or persons unknown."

◆

While it has been acknowledged from as far back as the time of the murders that there was the 'Canonical five' victims – Polly Nichols, Annie Chapman, Liz Stride, Catherine Eddowes and Mary Kelly – who many believe to be true Ripper victims, others have since questioned this. Over the years there have been up to 18 different women put forward in one way or another as a Jack the Ripper victim.

We strongly believe Martha Tabram was a victim of Jack the Ripper – probably his first victim. The lack of mutilation and minor inconsistencies are compatible with a killer refining his methods.

Polly Nichols, Annie Chapman, Catherine Eddowes and Mary Kelly also fit in with our belief they were true victims of Jack the Ripper. We believe that no man could commit the savagery and butchery they did with Mary Kelly and then contentedly go back to cutting throats and minor mutilations, even if it could strengthen our case against Jacob Levy, which we detail in the next chapter.

While it does seem unlikely another killer was at large in the area murdering women with knives, the actual truth does seem that they were just unfortunate victims of murder, a knife being a common weapon used in everyday life in Victorian London.

As for the other victims mentioned, it's highly likely that Emma Smith was attacked by a gang of men as she mentioned in her account of the attack.

Due to the errors and lack of information made in the initial investigation into the death of Rose Mylett, we feel she is the hardest to say whether or not she was a victim of Jack the Ripper. From the information available though, we believe she was probably strangled by someone and it not being a case of accidental death, although we don't believe it was Jack.

The next victim, Alice McKenzie, had cuts to her throat but these were neither long enough or deep enough to convince us they were the work of Jack. The mutilations were also mainly superficial, and in no way characteristic of those inflicted on the others.

Finally there was Frances Coles, who had no mutilations, and her throat had been cut using a blunt knife. We believe it's likely she was killed by the last client she was with; the one fellow prostitute Ellen Callana tried to warn her about after he had punched her when she refused his solicitation advances.

It's a sad fact that the only reason these poor women were ever mentioned was because of the proximity to Whitechapel, and the hysteria sweeping the streets created by Jack the Ripper.

11

JACOB LEVY: THE SUSPECT

Jacob Levy was brought to our attention quite a few years ago, when Mark King hypothesised in issue 26 of *Ripperologist* magazine (December 1999) how interesting it would be if the Mitre Square witness Joseph Hyam Levy and suspect Jacob Levy were related. We agreed, and set out to find if they could indeed be related, spending many years researching Jacob's family history in order to verify the link between him and Joseph Hyam Levy, and to prove our theory that Jacob was a valid suspect in the Jack the Ripper case.

Through our research, generations of the Levy family were traced (see Appendix II). The earliest verified record is that of Jacob's grandfather Isaac ben Hayim Levy (Isaac, son of Hyam Levy), who was born around 1770. We have located a Hyam Levy who was a butcher living at 49 Petticoat Lane in 1780. While it cannot be said for certain it's highly likely, given the occupation, name and address, that this was Isaac's father (and Jacob's great grandfather).

Sarah, Isaac's wife, was born in Holland in 1777. They had six children: Hyam (b.1810), Esther (b.1812), Elias (b.1816), Moss (b.1818), Joseph (b.1821) and Elizabeth (b.1826).

Hyam's birth certificate shows parents Isaac Levy, whose Jewish name was Yitzak, and Sarah living on Petticoat Lane, later renamed Middlesex

Street; a street where the family would remain for more than 80 years.

Petticoat Lane was famous for its markets. It was originally known as Hogg's Lane, way back before the 1500s. This could stem from the farmers taking their pigs to market, or due to the bakers keeping their pigs out in the streets. The name was changed to Petticoat Lane in the 17th century; the earliest mention is in 1600, when it was called Peticote Lane. It was at this time that market traders started to sell their clothes and other apparel there. The name was changed again around 1830 to Middlesex Street. It's a common misconception that this was because the prudish Victorians did not like the name of women's undergarments being spoken so freely, however this is not the case. It was in actual fact changed before the Victorian era – in the reign of William IV, and it was to record the boundary between Portsoken Ward, in the City of London and Whitechapel. It was now known as Middlesex Street, the name it is still known as today.

Underhill's Trennal Business Directory showed that Isaac registered his butchery business from that address in 1822; an occupation that would pass from generation to generation within the Levy family.

In 1836 Hyam Levy applied for the Freedom of the City, his application showing him as being 26-years-old, a butcher living at 41½ Petticoat Lane. His father is recorded as Isaac Levy, British-born but now deceased. Isaac's exact date of death cannot be pinpointed, but it was probably between 1831 and 1832, according to the land tax records on Ancestry.com.

In the 1841 census Sarah Levy was recorded as the head of the household at 38 Petticoat Lane, now a widow. Living with her at the time were sons Elias, Moss and Joseph, along with her daughter Elizabeth. It's interesting to note that Sarah was classed as a butcher; this seems to be an odd occupation for a woman in 1841. Looking through the census at that time in the immediate area, not many females were recorded as having any job at all, and those that did seem to be mainly servants or tailoresses.

The 1841 census shows that Hyam Levy, Isaac and Sarah's son, had taken over his father's butchery business at 36 Petticoat Lane. He had

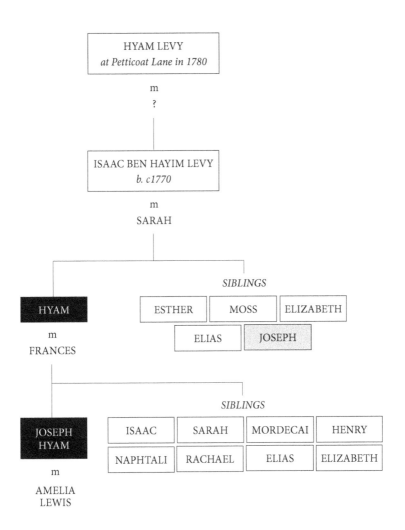

married Frances Naphtali on 31st December 1834 and was the father of three children, Isaac (b.1836), Naphtali (b.1838) and Sarah (b.1840).

The 1851 census shows Hyam's mother Sarah as still living at 38 Petticoat Lane. She was by now 74-years-old, but still listed as a butcher. Living with her were her sons Elias and Moss, and also one Morris Naphtali and his wife Maria. Morris was brother to Frances Levy, Hyam's wife.

Hyam and Frances were still living at 36 Petticoat Lane in the 1851 census, with their children Isaac, Napthali, Sarah, Joseph Hyam, Elias and Henry. Living at the same address was Hyam's mother-in-law, Leah Napthali. This census saw the first record for Joseph Hyam Levy, who had been born in 1842.

By 1861 Sarah Levy had moved out of 38 Petticoat Lane and was living as a boarder with Morris and Maria Naphtali at 23 Hutchinson Avenue. She was no longer carrying on the trade of butcher, and is in fact recorded as having no trade. There are no more records for Sarah, so it is highly likely that she died between the 1861 and 1871 censuses.

Hyam was still trading as a butcher from 36 Petticoat Lane in the 1861 census, together with Frances and their children Sarah, Elias, Elizabeth and Joseph Hyam, although in 1866 Joseph Hyam Levy moved out and married Amelia Lewis at the Great Synagogue. In the 1871 census he and Amelia were living at 1 Hutchinson Avenue, and his occupation was recorded as a butcher.

Joseph Hyam Levy's parents were still living at 36 Middlesex Street in the 1871 census along with their daughters Sarah and Elizabeth, although the following year Hyam Levy, Joseph Hyam's father, died at his home on 25th November after a painful illness lasting 40 hours, according to a newspaper article chronicling his death which appeared in *The Jewish Victorian 1871-1880*. In his Will he left everything to his wife Frances:

22 September 1873

Will of Hyam Levy – Effect under £100
The will of Hyam Levy late of 36 Middlesex Street, St Botolph,

JOSEPH
HYAM
LEVY'S
SHOP

MIDDLESEX STREET (OLD PETTICOAT LANE). 3490

Middlesex Street looking north;
Joseph Hyam Levy's shop at 1 Hutchinson Street indicated by arrow

Aldgate in the City of London, Butcher who died 25 November 1872
at Middlesex Street was proved at the Principal Registry by Frances
Levy of 36 Middlesex Street, widow of the relict the sole executrix.

With Frances widowed, in the 1881 census she was classed as head of
the household at 36 Middlesex Street. She seems to have taken over the
business after Hyam's death, as at the age of 72 she was now listed as a
butcher. Her daughters Sarah and Elizabeth were still living with her,
probably until their mother's death at the end of 1888, an event which
was recorded in the *Jewish Chronicle* of 4th January 1889:

> *Mr J.H. Levy of 1 Hutchinson Street and sisters return thanks for*
> *letters and condolences for their late lamented mother, Frances Levy,*
> *widow of the late Hyam Levy formerly of 36 Middlesex Street East.*

By the time of the 1891 census Sarah and Elizabeth were living at 4
Hutchinson Street. Sarah was listed as a housekeeper, and Elizabeth

a tailoress. It seems the following year Elizabeth married a man with the surname 'Jacobs' and had a son, Abraham, who was born on 13th February 1893. Unfortunately, there is no record found so far to identify her husband's first name. However if we look at the 1901 census we notice that there is a family named Jacobs living at 5 Hutchinson Avenue. Interesting, given Elizabeth married a Jacobs. Delving further back into this family's history we find that Harriet Jacobs living at 5 Hutchinson Avenue married a Joseph Jacobs, who had a brother Abraham born 1850 and died 1897. Going with this, we believe it's highly likely that Abraham Jacobs, the son, was named after Abraham Jacobs and the family living next door were aunts and cousins. While we acknowledge on one of his school intake records his father was named Phillip, this could in fact be his stepfather Phillip Goldberg, whom Elizabeth married in June 1904.

Some confusion stands over Joseph and his properties. Although it is verified that he was living at 1 Hutchinson Avenue in the 1871 census, according to the *City Directories* of 1870 he was living at 1 Hutchinson Street, trading as a butcher, and again in 1875.

So either Joseph Hyam Levy lived at 1 Hutchinson Street in 1870, moved to 1 Hutchinson Avenue by the time of the 1871 census and then moved back to 1 Hutchinson Street by 1875, or he owned both properties, or there was a mistake with the 1871 census. What we do know is that he was still living at 1 Hutchinson Street in 1881, and in 1891 he was still living there, working as a butcher. Records show he still resided at that address in 1893, but by 1898 he was recorded as living at 124 Mildmay Road in Islington, just a few houses away from his friend Joseph Lawende who lived at 140 Mildmay Road.

Joseph Hyam and Amelia were still living in Mildmay Road in 1911. Amelia died on 4th September 1912. A *Jewish Chronicle* death notice dated 6th September 1912 read:

> On the 4th September 1912 at Brighton, Milly, the beloved wife of J. H. Levy, 124 Mildmay Road N, may her soul rest in peace.

Another notice in the *Jewish Chronicle* of the same date gave a little more information:

On the 4th September, at Brighton, after a sad and long illness, Amelia, wife of J. H. Levy, and beloved sister of Henry and Moss Lewis, 12, Howitt Road, Belsize Park N.W.

Joseph Hyam Levy himself died four years later, in May 1916. His will showed he was a generous man:

Mr Joseph Hyam Levy, of 124 Mildmay Road, Mildmay Park, who died on May 16th, and whose will is proved by Harry Moss, of 23 Wormwood Street, and Joseph Barnett of 292, Old Ford Road, has left £2,410 11s 6d. He gave his wearing apparel to the Jewish Homes for the Incurables; £200 to his sister Elizabeth Goldberg; £100 to Abraham Jacobs; £100 to Alfred Levy; £100 to Fanny Levy; £30 to Ted Levy; and the proceeds of the sale of the Hutchinson Street property to his sister, Elizabeth Goldberg, after the payment of £100 to Alfred Levy. The residue of the property is to be divided between St. Peter's Hospital, London Hospital, Jewish Hospital, German Hospital, Home and Hospital for Jewish Incurables, Home for the aged Jews, Jews' Hospital and Orphans Asylum, Victoria Park Hospital, Opthalmic Hospital, City Road, Alderman Treloar's Cripples Home, and the Jewish Blind Society.

◆

Moving to the other branch of the family tree, Hyam Levy's brother Joseph had been living with their parents in the 1841 census, and had also followed his family's trade as a butcher.

We don't know the exact date that Joseph left 38 Petticoat Lane to set up home with a widow named Caroline Solomons, but we do know it was between 1846 and 1847 as Caroline had two children, Rebecca and Jane, from her previous marriage to Joshua Solomons, who had died from phthisis on 22nd March 1846. The address on his death certificate was 5 Love Court.

On 14th September 1847 Hannah Levy was born, the address on the birth certificate was 5 Love Court. This showed that Joseph and Caroline were living together prior to their marriage in the third quarter of 1848 and subsequent move to 4 Little Middlesex Street, where they are recorded in the 1851 census. Living there with them at that time were Caroline's daughters Rebecca and Jane, and also Joseph and Caroline's children, Hannah and Elizabeth.

By the 1861 census the family had moved around the corner to 111 Middlesex Street. Joseph was still working as a butcher. With them were their children Jane, Hannah, Elizabeth, Isaac, Abraham, Moses and five-year-old Jacob. This was the first census record listing Jacob Levy, who was born 11th March 1856.

In 1871 Jacob, now fifteen-years-old, and was living at the same address with his parents and siblings. He was no longer recorded as a scholar, but as a butcher following what was evidently a family business – his grandmother, grandfather, uncles, cousin, father and brother were all recorded as butchers over the generations. This occupation would have provided Jacob with the required knife skills and basic anatomical knowledge needed to kill and mutilate the Whitechapel victims.

The above shows that Joseph Hyam Levy and Jacob Levy were without doubt first cousins. They were also in the same trade – butchery – and lived very close to each other. Jacob Levy would eventually buy the house and business that Joseph Hyam Levy grew up in.

Life changed for the Levy family in 1875, when Jacob's elder brother Abraham committed suicide at the age of 22, as reported in the *Lloyd's Weekly London News* of 28th May 1875:

SUICIDE ON DERBY DAY

Suicides -Yesterday Mr Humphreys, the coroner for the Eastern Division of Middlesex, received information of the death of Abraham Levy, aged 22 years, carrying on the business of a butcher at 111, Middlesex Street, Whitechapel. Deceased had bet heavily on the races, and on arrival of the news he appeared very desponding. At a quarter-past six the door of his bed-room was found to be locked, and on its being burst open he was discovered suspended by a rope which he had fastened round his neck to the door. A doctor was called in, but life had been extinct some time. On account of the Jewish custom an inquest will be held on this day (Friday).

JACOB LEVY: THE SUSPECT

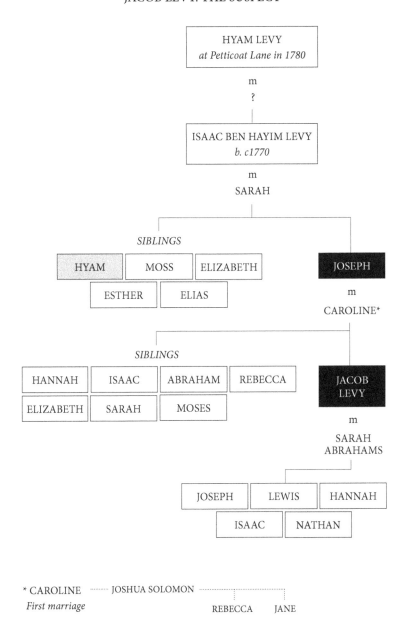

Newspaper reports such as the following from the *Glasgow Herald* of 28th May 1875 showed that Jacob (recorded as 'Joseph', the Jewish version of his name) was the person who found his brother hanging from the ceiling:

RESULTS OF UNFORTUNATE SPECULATION

On Friday, Mr. Humphries held an inquest at the Coach and Horses, Middlesex Street, Whitechapel, on the body of Abraham Levy, aged 22, who committed suicide on Derby night. The evidence proved that the deceased, the son of a butcher, lived at 111 Middlesex Street. On Wednesday evening, shortly after 6pm, he left the shop and went up to his room for the purpose of dressing, but nothing being heard of him, suspicions were aroused, when one Joseph Levy, brother to the deceased, going up he found the door locked. After repeated kickings, and no answer being given, the door was burst open, when he was discovered suspended by a rope line from the neck to a nail which he had fastened in the wall.

The jury returned a verdict of "Suicide whilst of unsound mind".

The Jewish custom that no person who had committed suicide could be buried in consecrated ground was not adhered to if the person did so whilst of unsound mind. Due to this clause, Abraham was allowed to be buried in West Ham Cemetery, where his parents would eventually be buried, instead of land specifically designated outside of consecrated grounds at the Jewish synagogues.

The Jewish Victorian by Doreen Berger, which collates genealogical information from Jewish newspapers between 1871 and 1880 recorded the following:

ABRAHAM LEVY

The tombstone to the memory of ABRAHAM LEVY, son of JOSEPH LEVY, Butcher, of 111 Middlesex Street, Whitechapel, will be set 15 August, 1875 at West Ham.

So here we have a 19-year-old Jacob frantically battering down his bedroom door to find his brother hanging by a rope, probably with a bloated face, a protruding tongue and bulging eyes staring back at him. This was his brother, just two years older than him; they grew up, fought, laughed, cried and shared a life together.

◆

In business listings for 1878 given in the *Jewish Chronicle* which supply the names and addresses of those licensed to supply kosher meat and poultry to the Jewish community, Jacob Levy is noted at 11 Fieldgate Street. This seems to have been his work address, for when he married Sarah Abrahams the following year, on 23rd April 1879, the marriage record makes it clear that he was actually still living at 111 Middlesex Street.

The wedding certificate records Jacob as a 23-year-old bachelor, a butcher living at 111 Middlesex Street. His father's name was Joseph Levy, and he was also a butcher. The bride was Sarah Abrahams, a spinster aged 22. She had no given occupation, and was also living at 111 Middlesex Street. Her father's name was Isaac Abrahams, a tailor.

They were still in Fieldgate Street in 1881. In the census of that year he was listed as Joseph Levy, the only other time that he used this name besides at the inquest into his brother's suicide. Jacob now had two sons, Joseph born 17th August 1879 and Isaac, born 15th January 1881. His occupation was again that of a butcher.

1883 saw the deaths of some of Jacob's relatives. On 26th October an article appeared in The *Jewish Chronicle* referring to Nathan Hyams, who was husband to Rebecca Solomons, Jacob's half-sister:

SAD DEATH

On Tuesday [23rd October] the City Coroner Mr Payne held an inquest at the Coroner's Court, Golden Lane, on the body of Nathan Hyams, aged 49, a fishmonger, lately dwelling in Sandy's Row, Bishopsgate. Deceased, it appeared, had been very unfortunate in business, and was in such reduced circumstances that he could scarcely maintain himself and family. They had suffered a great deal of privation, and their condition preyed very much upon the deceased's mind. On Friday morning last, his son found him hanging by the neck by a rope, which was fastened to the banisters of the stairs. Medical evidence was given that death resulted from strangulation, and the jury returned a verdict to the effect that the deceased committed suicide while temporarily insane.

A short time later, Jacob's cousin Naphtali Levy also died:

The tombstone in memory of the late Naphtali Levy of 111 Mile End Road, will be set on SUNDAY, Dec 30th, at West Ham Cemetery, at 3pm. Relatives and friends please accept this intimation.

Between 1883 and 1884 Jacob took over the butchering business of his aunt Frances Levy at 36 Middlesex Street. This had been her home since her marriage to Hyam in 1837, and also Jacob's grandparents' home since at least 1810, where it is noted on the birth record for Hyam. In this year Jacob and Sarah had another child, Lewis born on 20th January, and in 1885 welcomed Hannah.

On 10th March 1886 Jacob was arrested by PC Bacon for being involved in the theft of meat from his neighbour Hyman Sampson. His appearance in court came a few weeks later, on 5th April 1886, and was recorded in the Old Bailey transcript:

Morris Phillips (30), Moss Woolf (16), and Jacob Levy (30), stealing 14lb of meat of Hyman Sampson, the master of Phillips and Woolf.

Mr Clure prosecuted; Mr Moyser appeared for Phillips, Mr Black for Woolf and Mr Geoghegan for Levy.

Samuel Bacon (City Policeman 941): I received information from my Inspector, and on 10th of March, at 6.15 am, I was watching the prosecutor's shop. Phillips came up to the door and knocked, got no answer, and went away. About two minutes afterwards Levy came out at his shop door, which is next door, a post divides them. Then he knocked at Mr Sampson's door and went back in at his own door, came out again in a minute or two, unscrewed the bolt of the shutter bar, and then looked around and knocked at Mr Sampson's door again; there being no answer he went down the street 10 or 12 yards to the corner of Stoney Lane. Phillips joined him; they conversed and

Middlesex Street looking south, the junction with Stoney Lane plastered with advertisements on the right. No. 36, home to Jacob Levy, obscured by the streetlamp.

went back to Mr Sampson's door. Phillips knocked, and Levy went in at his own door. The door was opened; Phillips went in and turned up the gas. Levy came out of his shop and went into Mr Sampson's shop, where he had a conversation with Phillips. He came back in about a minute and went into his own shop, where I saw Woolf, who brought a piece of meat from the back of the shop to the door, and hung it on a hook just inside the door, and then came out on the footway, looked round, took the meat off the hook and took it quickly in at Lewis's [sic], and gave it to Lewis [sic], he then returned to Samson's shop. I ran into Levy's shop, got hold of him with the meat in his hand, and asked what he was going to do with it. He said "We are only having a laugh, I am going to weigh it." I said I did not believe it, I should take him to Mr Sampson, which I did, and then took him to the station, where he repeated that it was only a lark. I found £32 10s 9d in his *pocket. The meat was 14lb of beef. I had been watching since 5.15 am; it was perfectly light outside at 6:15, but not inside Levy's shop, there being no gas.*

Cross-examined by Mr Black: I was in some buildings opposite, lying among some bricks and rubbish, but not within hearing distance. I could not see who opened the door as the shutters were not down, but Phillips turned the gas up afterwards. We were both in plain clothes. Woolf sleeps on the premises.

Cross-examined by Mr Geoghegan: I cannot say whether these men are rival butchers; they are both Jews. When he said he did it for a lark Mr Sampson said "You will be locked up for it." He valued the meat at 6d per lb. This is Petticoat Lane, and there are other butchers in the street. It was about the time a man would go to market.

James Jones (City policeman 935): I was with Bacon; I have heard his evidence and corroborate it. I went into Sampson's shop, and saw Phillips und [sic] Woolf; I told them I was a police officer, and should take them in custody for stealing a piece of beef. Phillips said "I know nothing about it, I came from the back of the shop." Woolf said "I know nothing about it." I took them to the station.

Cross-examined by Mr Black: Woolf did not say "I know nothing about it," I correct myself, he made no reply.

Cross-examined by Mr Geoghegan: I did not go into Levy's shop, nor did I see in, as the shutters were up. There may have been a quantity of meat in the background.

Hyman Sampson: I am a butcher of 35 Middlesex Street. Phillips and Woolf were my servants; Phillips about three months, and Woolf about two or two and a half years. I had spoken to the police, and on the 10th of March about 5 o'clock I went to the market. I was sent for, and came back and found the three prisoners in custody. The policeman asked Levy what he intended to do with it, he said that the boy brought it for a lark, and then said "Mr Sampson, you are not going to do anything with me." The meat was worth 7s.

Cross-examined by Mr Moyser: Phillips slept at the shop on Wednesdays and Thursdays, this was Wednesday morning. He would sleep away from the shop on Tuesday nights.

Cross-examined by Mr Black: I discharged Woolf once and took him

*back again. I had a place in Goldstone Street [sic] for nineteen years.
I know Binwell, a butcher, I took Woolf from his employment. I never
asked for a character, he was only a little boy, I have never found fault
with him before.*

*Cross-examined by Mr Geoghegan: Levy was there before I came. He
has not taken customers from me. I have no animosity against him.
I have met him out of business hours. This was not the best meat at
6d a pound. I have some at 11d. Levy has never chaffed me and said
that his meat was better than mine, he buys from the same killer I do.
I sell more expensive meat than he does, but there has been no joking
about, nor did we ever bet about it. The Jewish authorities will not
give a man a licence unless he has excellent character. I have accused
my wife of robbing me. I did not find out that she had a separate
banking account. I did not accuse her before Phillips came into my
service. I may have said at the police court that I accused her 12
months ago. I have not said that if Levy would leave his shop I would
not carry on the prosecution against him. I would not let him off for
£10,000.*

Re-examined. At 6.15 am my five employees were on the premises.

Levy received a good character.

PHILLIPS – Not guilty.

*WOOLF – Guilty. Recommended to mercy by the jury. Four months'
Hard Labour.*

LEVY – Guilty of receiving – Twelve months' Hard Labour.

In summation, Jacob stole seven shillings' worth of inferior meat,
which even by Hyman Sampson's own admission was not one of his best
cuts. Court transcripts show he had £32 10s 9d on him when arrested,
which would have amounted to £2,153.48 in today's money. Back in
1886 this would have been the equivalent of 98 days' wages for a skilled
worker, so it is obvious that Jacob didn't steal the meat for monetary
gain.

It is possible that Jacob had indeed done it for a 'lark' and Hyman
Sampson used this as an excuse to get rid of a rival businessman.
However, if this was the case it seems a little odd that he would actively

involve a policeman and lose any leverage he had over Jacob. Another explanation could be the onset of his mental decline, which manifested itself in him committing the theft without any forethought of the ramifications.

Just nine days after the arrest, on 19th March, Jacob's father died from intestinal obstruction and exhaustion. The doctor who certified Joseph's death was in fact the same doctor who would send Jacob to the asylum just a few short years later – Dr Henry Sequeira.

Jacob was sent first to Holloway Prison, and then transferred to Chelmsford Prison on 19th April to serve his sentence. However, a few weeks later, on 21st May, Jacob was certified insane after an attempting suicide, and was admitted to Essex County Lunatic Asylum at Chelmsford on 26th May 1886.

While Jacob was in the asylum Sarah gave birth to another son, Nathan, born on 8th June 1886.

The admission records from Essex Asylum recorded that Jacob was married and had four children, although he didn't know the age of the youngest child. His occupation was noted as a butcher and his state of bodily health was described as 'Good.' It was recorded by medical staff that this was his first attack, and that it had lasted about three weeks. Jacob was described as suicidal, the cause being that he was 'Fretting about business and family'.

The heading 'Chief delusions or indication of insanity' comes under two parts. The first part was to be written by the Medical Officer himself, recording his observations of the patient. The second part was for observation made by others. For his part, the Medical Officer E.H. Carter noted that Jacob was 'rambling and incoherent talking, restlessness and insomnia.'

The second part of the form was recorded by Temporary Warder Wade, whose comments on Jacob were noted on how he had attempted suicide by strangling, 'shouting restless and talking at night. Violence. Incessantly talking of imaginary people.'

The document was dated 26th May 1886 and was signed by Medical Officer Dr Carter.

STATEMENT respecting Criminal Lunatics, to be filled up and transmitted to the
Medical Superintendent with every Criminal Lunatic.

A newspaper report of trial should also be forwarded, if procurable.

Name	*Jacob Levy*
Age	*30*
Date of admission	*Convicted 5 ap 1886. (Transferred to Chelmsford Prison 19.4.86)*
Former occupation	*Butcher*
From whence brought	*Holloway Prison*
Married, single, or widower	*Married*
How many children	*4*
Age of youngest	*Unknown*
Whether first attack	*Yes*
When previous attacks occurred	
Duration of existing attack	*About three weeks*
State of bodily health	*good.*

[OVER.

*Record of Jacob Levy's transferral from Chelmsford Prison to
Essex County Lunatic Asylum on 26th May 1886.*

119

Another document from the admission file from Chelmsford has a handwritten explanation of Jacob's state of mind at that time:

> *He is in a state of melancholia, cries without adequate cause – is very despondent from the fact that he attempted suicide by strangulation at Gaol and that a brother committed suicide and insanity is hereditary is in his family. I consider him suicidal and insane. He is in fair health and condition.*

This report was dated 3rd June 1886, signed 'G. A.'

This is a breakdown of epic proportions.

Now, let's be critical; on 5th April Jacob is a husband, father and employer in a thriving business. Just twenty eight days later he is basically a gibbering wreck, suicidal, violent and depressed, yet physically healthy. Surely there must be some background mental aberration for this, some illness, and yet there is no mention of syphilis.

Could it have anything to do with the death of his father?

Another form from Jacob's time at Chelmsford, dated 31st January 1887, is a handwritten letter addressed to the Superintendent of the County Asylum at Brentwood Essex, which states:

> *Sir, I am directed by the Secretary of State to acknowledge the receipt of your letter dated 22nd instance enclosing a certificate for the criminal lunatic Jacob Levy is now of sound mind and fit for discharge; and I am to transmit to you, herewith, under all the circumstances of the case, a warrant authorising his absolute discharge, under section 5 of the criminal lunatic act 1884 from your asylum.*
>
> *I am sir, your obedient servant, Godfrey Lushington.*

The Warrant of Absolute Discharge includes Jacob's registered criminal number, X10341. The reason and date of his conviction was stated as being for receiving stolen goods, on 5th April 1886. The register then states that he was sentenced to 12 calendar months with hard labour at Brentwood, and his sentence was to end on 25th May 1886.

Underneath this is another part, the Warrant of Absolute Discharge,

Record of Jacob Levy's Absolute Discharge, signed by Home Secretary Henry Matthews on 31st January 1887 which states 'This warrant is to authorise and require you to cause the Criminal Lunatic described above to be absolutely discharged.' It was signed by Henry Matthews, the Home Secretary, and dated 31st January 1887.

Jacob Levy was officially released two months earlier than his sentence was due to end, and so on 3rd February 1887 he returned home to 36 Middlesex Street. Eight short weeks later, on 2nd April, his persecutor Hyman Sampson, who was still residing at 35 Middlesex Street, died.

The death notice was placed in the *Jewish Chronicle* of Friday, 6th April 1887:

> *On 2nd April at 33 [sic] Middlesex Street Aldgate, after a long illness, Mr Hyman Sampson aged 63. Deeply lamented by his sorrowing wife and family May his soul rest in peace.*

The following month an article was placed in the *Jewish Chronicle*, of 13th May 1887:

> *The Tombstone in memory of the late HYMAN SAMPSON, of 35, Middlesex Street will be SET at West Ham Cemetery, on SUNDAY, the 15th inst., at 3 o'clock – Friends will kindly accept this the only intimation.*

On 14th October 1887 Jacob and Sarah welcomed another son into the family, Jacob Jr. He was born eight months after his father had entered the asylum.

By 1888 Jacob was still working and living at 36 Middlesex Street.

1888 saw another tragic death in Jacob's life, when his mother Caroline died on 18th May, as reported in the *Jewish Chronicle*:

18th May 1888 at 198 Wentworth Buildings, Caroline Levy, a female, 69 years old and widow of Joseph Levy Butcher, master, died of Cancer, 2 years, Bronchitis 1 year and 'haemorrhagic + collapse' ½ an hour. Certified by J.W.D. Long. The name of the informant was Isaac Levy, Son, of 214 Wentworth Buildings, Whitechapel.

It was the year of the horrific murders which forever immortalised the East End of London. It is likely that Jacob was questioned at least once, as it was recorded in a report by Chief Inspector Donald Swanson to the Home Office dated 19th October 1888 that butchers and slaughtermen were questioned in the area.

Following the murder of Catherine Eddowes in Mitre Square it was noticed that a portion of her apron had been sliced off and taken away, possibly to carry away body parts which were later discovered to be missing.

At 2.55am that morning, the missing piece of apron was found by PC Long in the entrance of a tenement block in Goulston Street known as Wentworth Model Dwellings, lying on the floor below the 'Juwes' graffiti. These were relatively new buildings, built in 1885, and had a slightly strange layout. The front blocks in Goulston Street were numbered 132-143, 120-131,108-119 (where the apron was found and the graffiti was

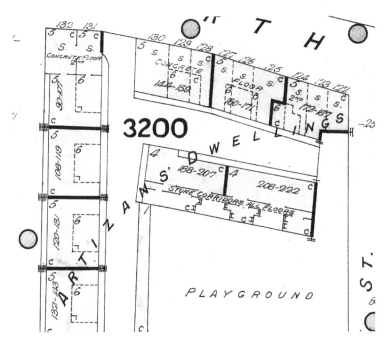

written on the wall) and 90-107. They continued on in an L-shape into Wentworth Street, numbered 144-159, 160-171 and 172-187. Behind these buildings were another two blocks numbered 188-207 and 208-222.

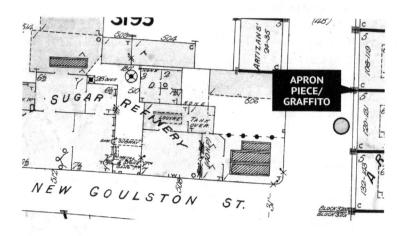

The diagram above shows the spot where the bloody apron piece was discarded. It was later proved to fit exactly that missing part of Catherine Eddowes' apron, leaving no doubt it was hers. No-one has been able to satisfactorily link the apron and graffiti to the place it was found – until now.

Jacob Levy lived in Middlesex Street, parallel to Goulston Street. By walking out of his home and turning right, he would quickly come to the junction with New Goulston Street, which ended at Goulston Street and directly opposite Wentworth Buildings. Diagonally crossing the road would have him directly outside the doorway where the apron piece and graffiti were found; he could make this walk in under two minutes.

Jacob's mother Caroline lived at 198 Wentworth Buildings at the time of her death, 11 weeks prior to the murder of Martha Tabram and 14 to the killing of Polly Nichols. The passageway of 108-119 Wentworth Model Dwellings was in a direct line with his mother's rooms. Slipping inside the entranceway, he could have dropped the apron piece. It's also

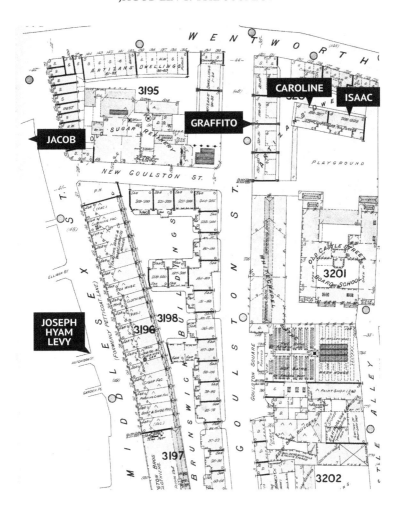

possible that he took out his butcher's chalk and wrote the infamous graffiti, as he surely had enough time. He could then continue walking through the passageway straight out the back of the building, to his mother's former residence. It's possible his mother's apartment was still empty, although given the cramped, overcrowded streets of Whitechapel this is not likely. Jacob's younger sister Rebecca was living with their mother in the 1881 census, aged twelve, she could still have been there, by now aged 19.

Living in the block next to Caroline's accommodation, at 214 Wentworth Buildings, was Jacob's brother Isaac Levy. We know he was there in 1888, as his daughter Rebecca was born there that year. The fact that he had at least two close relatives in such a close proximity to where the apron piece and graffiti were found could be explanation enough for Jacob to have been there.

It has been pointed out that on the Goad map of 1890 there is no exit at the rear of the buildings. But there are no front entrances either – in fact, there are no exits or entrances depicted at all. It does not mean they were not there.

At the inquest into Catherine Eddowes's death, Constable Long was questioned with regard to the discovery of the bloody apron:

> *Foreman of the Jury: "Was there any possibility of a stranger escaping from the house?"*
> *Constable Long: "Not from the front."*
> *Coroner: "Did you not know about the back?"*
> *Constable Long: "No, that was the first time I had been on duty there."*

Unfortunately, we can't find any information to fully corroborate whether there was a rear exit or not. We know by studying the history of the area that these tenement blocks were probably built by one of two companies, The Four Percent Company or East End Dwellings. We have contacted the Rothschild company, who owned The Four Percent Company, but they unfortunately have no records of the building. East End Dwellings are no longer in operation, but from research carried out there is no mention of Goulston Street tenements. Further research, however, does uncover a book by Joseph O'Neill titled *Secret World of the Victorian Lodging House*. In this he quite confidently states the following:

> *The East End vicar, the Reverend Barnett, founded the East London Company to buy and refurbish properties to provide decent housing*

for the poor. By 1886 he had established Brunswick Buildings and
Wentworth Buildings right in the heart of Spitalfields rookery...

The buildings on the opposite side of Goulston Street, Brunswick Buildings, were built around the same time as Wentworth Model Dwellings and they *did* have a rear exit, and while it's noted that East End Dwellings Company owned both properties and it's plausible they might be a mirror image of each other, with a lack of proper documentation for Wentworth Model Dwellings we can't say for certain whether these were of the same layout.

As to the graffiti, the significance of the words are not known. But if they were indeed written by the killer, then Jacob had the means to have done so. According to the asylum records, his level of education level was 'good' and he signed his own marriage certificate, so we know he had at least enough of an education to be able to read and write. It's also likely that he carried some butcher's chalk on him.

It was also very interesting to us that while doing our research we discovered that Hyman Sampson, whose testimony sent Jacob to prison and on to the asylum in 1886, had a dairy and butcher's shop in Goulston Street before moving to Middlesex Street in 1885. He moved because all the buildings on that side were demolished to make way for Wentworth Buildings. Hyman's shop was at No. 56 Goulston Street, which would

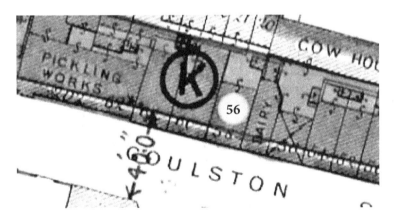

have been situated right in the area at which the apron piece and graffiti were found.

Coincidence?

In 1890 Jacob returned to an insane asylum, this time Stone House Hospital, formerly the City of London Lunatic Asylum in Kent. The first paper in his file is a letter titled the Certificate of Medical Practitioner Form, and it explains how and why Jacob had been sent to the asylum:

> *In the matter of Jacob Levy of 36 Middlesex Street Aldgate E in the City of London, Butcher an alleged lunatic.*
>
> *I the undersigned Henry James Sequeira do hereby certify as follows:-*
> *I am the person registered under the Medical Act of 1858, and I am in the actual practice of the medical profession.*
>
> *On the 14th day of August 1890 at 36 Middlesex Street Aldgate E in the City of London, I personally examined the said Jacob Levy and came to the conclusion that he is a person of unsound mind and a proper person to be taken charge of and detained under care and treatment. I formed this conclusion on the following grounds viz;-*
> *Facts indicating insanity observed by myself at the time of examination viz*
>
> *Known patient several years, formerly shrewd businessman, now quite incapable of earning on same. Giving wrong change and money back for things bought. Says he feels a something within him, impelling him to take everything he sees. Feels that if he is not restrained he will do some violence to someone. Complains of hearing strange noises.*
>
> *Facts communicated by others viz:-*
> *Sarah Levy, 36 Middlesex Street, wife, deposes – That he has nearly ruined her business, being quite incapable of taking care of money, making away with every penny he can put his hands on. Orders goods indiscriminately and is continually taking other people's goods, carrying them off. Wanders away from home for hours without any purpose. Does not sleep at night, raves he is continually fancying someone is going to do him bodily harm.*
>
> *The said Jacob Levy appeared to me to be in a fit condition of bodily health to be removed to an asylum, hospital or licensed house.*
>
> *I give this certificate having first read the section of the Act of*

Particulars of Jacob Levy's admission to Stone House Hospital

CERTIFICATE OF MEDICAL PRACTITIONER.—Form 8.

In the matter of _Jacob Levy_

(a) *[marginal note]* of (a). 36 Middlesex Street Aldgate E.

(b) *[marginal note]* in the (b) City of London

(c) *[marginal note]* (c) Butcher

an alleged lunatic.

I, the undersigned _Henry James Sequeira_

do hereby certify as follows:—

1. I am a person registered under the Medical Act, 1858, and I am in the actual practice of the medical profession.

2. On the _14ᵗʰ_ day of _August_ 1890, at (d) _36 Middlesex Street, Aldgate E_ in the (c) _City_ of _London_ I personally examined the said _Jacob Levy_ and came to the conclusion that he is (f) _person of unsound mind_ and a proper person to be taken charge of and detained under care and treatment.

3. I formed this conclusion on the following grounds, viz.:—

(a) Facts indicating insanity observed by myself at the time of examination (g) viz.

[handwritten] Known patient several years formerly shrewd business man, now quite incapable of carrying on same, giving wrong change & money back for things bought. Says he feels a something within him, impelling him to take everything he sees, felt that if he is not restrained he will do some violence to some one. Complains of hearing strange noises.

(b) Facts communicated by others (h) viz.—

[handwritten, marginal: Wife (Sarah Levy) 36 Middlesex St] Deposes:— That he has nearly ruined the business, being quite incapable of taking care of money. That is away with every penny he can put his hand on. Orders goods indiscriminately & is continually taking other people's goods, carrying them off. Wanders away from home for hours without any purpose. Does not sleep at night, rave & is continually fancying someone is going to do him bodily harm.

4. The said _Jacob Levy_ appeared to me to be [or not to be] in a fit condition of bodily health to be removed to an asylum, hospital, or licensed house. (i)

5. I give this certificate having first read the section of the Act of Parliament printed below.

Dated this _Fourteenth_ day of _August_ 1890.

(Signed) _H. J. Sequeira_

of (k) _34 Jewry Street Aldgate London E._

Extract from section 317 of the Lunacy Act, 1890.

Any person who makes a wilful misstatement of any material fact in any medical or other certificate or in any statement or report of bodily or mental condition under this Act, shall be guilty of a misdemeanor.

LUNACY 8.

Dr Henry Sequeira's examination notes

Parliament printed below.
Dated this fourteenth date August 1890
Signed H.J. Sequeira of 34 Jewry Street Aldgate London E.

So on 14th August 1890 Sarah requested that Dr Henry Sequeira of 34 Jewry Street, brother to George William Sequeira who attended the scene of Catherine Eddowes' murder, examine Jacob at his home, 36 Middlesex Street. This was the same doctor who had signed the death certificate of Jacob's father in 1886. On examination, Dr Sequeira declared that Jacob was of unsound mind and needed to be placed in an insane asylum.

The next paper is titled The Relieving Officer of the Poor Law Union in the City of London:

Whereas I the undersigned, and one of Her Majesty's Justices of the Peace in and for the City of London on the 14th day of August received notice from you that Jacob Levy, a person chargeable to the City of London Union, is deemed to be a person of unsound mind.

I therefore hereby order and require you to bring the said Jacob Levy before me, on the 15th day of August in the year of our Lord One Thousand Eight Hundred and Ninety at Eleven o'clock in the forenoon, at Guildhall Justice room in the said city or before such other Justice of the Peace for the said [City] as may then be there to be dealt with according to Law.

Given under my Hand and Seal, at the Guildhall Justice Room in the said City, this 14th day of August in the year of our Lord, One Thousand Eight Hundred and Ninety.

Signed
James Whitehead.

Included in the admission file for Stone is another paper dated 14th August 1890, titled Order for a Pauper Lunatic Wandering at Large:

I, George Robert Tyler, Esquire, being an Alderman and Justice of the Peace of the City of London having called to my assistance Henry James Sequeira of 34 Jewry Street Aldgate, a duly qualified medical practitioner and being satisfied that Jacob Levy of 36 Middlesex Street Aldgate is a pauper in receipt of relief and that the said Jacob Levy is a person of unsound mind and a proper person to be taken charge hereby direct you to receive the said Jacob Levy as a patient into your asylum. Subjoined is a statement of particulars respecting the said Jacob Levy and I hereby require you Walter Boscher a Relieving officer forthwith to convey the Lunatic aforementioned to the Institution herein named.

Signed

George Robert Tyler Esquire.

Within the file is a record of financial transactions, with the charges for the examination and diagnosis of Jacob and transport required given:

The Guardians of the City of London Union W. Boscher Relieving Officer re Jacob Levy (a Lunatic)

Expense incurred on conveying the above named person from 36 Middlesex Street to Guildhall therein to Stone, City of London Lunatic Asylum.

Stamps at Guildhall 5.6

Cab fare to Justice Room 7-

Railway fare (Special compt) 10.4

Cab fare at Dartford 3.6

Expenses for patient and attendant and R.O 7.6

Total expenses £1.8.10

Records show that monies owed to Dr Sequeira was 1 guinea for his examination of Jacob, and £1 8s 10d to Walter Boscher for taking him to the Guildhall.

The Statement of Particulars that followed consisted of standard information: Jacob Levy, 34, married, a butcher, Hebrew persuasion, residing at 36 Middlesex Street. It also noted that it wasn't his first attack, having had one when he was 30-years-old at Essex County Asylum in 1886. The duration of the attack was 'some time', and the supposed cause was not known. Whether epileptic, dangerous or suicidal; all are answered 'No'.

The next comment was very interesting. When asked whether any near relative had been afflicted with insanity, Jacob answered yes – his elder brother had **cut his throat**. [authors' emphasis]

As Jacob had only two elder brothers – Isaac and Abraham – and Isaac didn't die until 1901, this leaves Abraham, who we know committed suicide in 1875 by hanging himself with a rope; a very different method than cutting his own throat, as Jacob claimed. Could this just be yet another coincidence, or had Jacob developed a fixation with cutting throats?

Jacob's admission records give us a little insight to the sort of person he was. The first page shows his name, age, occupation and address, but it also says he was physically quite healthy. He was described as not being epileptic, suicidal or dangerous. His education was classified as 'Good' and his religious persuasion as 'Hebrew'. At the bottom of the page there was also a copy of the report and deposition of Dr Sequeira and Sarah Levy gave on Dr Sequeira's medical report.

Jacob was described as being covered with scratches, also deeply discoloured with a copper colour, most likely syphilitic, and he also had wounds on his right buttock and left index finger, and two marks of recent boils on his back.

His height and weight were recorded as at 5ft 3in and 9st 3lb.

As stated in his intake records, Jacob suffered from syphilis. Syphilis is known to be an infectious venereal disease caused by the spirochetal bacterium *Treponema* subspecies *pallidum*. If untreated it progresses through four stages – primary, secondary, latent and tertiary. One of the nicknames for syphilis is 'the great imposter', due to the fact that it mimics many other infections. Sir William Osler remarked, 'The physician who knows syphilis knows medicine.'

Syphilis can either be acquired through sexual contact, congenitally or, more rarely, through blood transfusions. When contracting syphilis, the *T pallidum* penetrates intact mucous membranes or microscopic dermal abrasions, and within a few hours it has entered the lymphatic and blood to produce a systematic infection. Incubation time from

Jacob Levy's medical notes at Stone House Asylum

exposure to the development of primary lesions averages around three weeks, but it can range from anything between ten and ninety days.

The central nervous system is infected early in the illness, normally at the secondary stage. During the first five to ten years after the onset of the untreated primary infection the disease principally involves the meninges and blood vessels, resulting in meningovascular neurosyphilis. Later the parenchyma of the brain and spinal cord are damaged, resulting in parenchymatous neurosyphilis.

Primary syphilis is characterised by the development of a painless chancre at the site of transmission after an incubation period of three to six weeks. The lesion is highly infectious, whether treated or not. Healing usually occurs within three to twelve weeks, although there may be residual scarring.

Secondary syphilis develops about four to ten weeks after the appearance of the primary lesion. During this stage, the spirochetes multiply and spread throughout the body. Secondary syphilis lesions vary in their manifestations. Symptoms may include malaise, fever, muscle and joint pain, swollen lymph nodes and rash. During secondary infection, the immune reaction is at its peak.

Latent syphilis follows on from the secondary stage, and if untreated the patient will go on to develop tertiary, from which neurosyphilis may occur. The three general categories of tertiary syphilis are gummatous syphilis (also called late benign), cardiovascular syphilis and neurosyphilis.

Neurosyphilis has several forms, which include tabes dorsalis and general paresis. Tabes dorsalis develops as the posterior columns and dorsal roots of the spinal cord are damaged. Posterior column impairment results in impaired vibration and proprioceptive sensation, leading to a wide-based gait, similar to a bow-legged walk. Disruption of the dorsal roots leads to loss of pain and temperature sensation and areflexia. Damage to the cortical regions of the brain leads to general paresis, formerly called 'general paresis of the insane,' which mimics other forms of dementia. Impairment of memory and speech, personality changes, irritability, and psychotic symptoms develop and may advance to progressive dementia. The Argyll Robertson pupil, which does not react to light but does constrict during accommodation, may be seen in tabes dorsalis and general paresis. The precise location of the lesion causing this phenomenon is unknown.

Jacob's medical notes give us an insight into his health and everyday life in the asylum. The first entry is dated 18th August 1890, and describes how he had recently taken to drink; how he used to be a good father and husband, but had become neglectful.

The next entry, dated 21st August, records that Jacob was suffering from mania and that he 'felt compelled to do acts contrary to the dictates of his conscience by a power which he cannot withstand.' Physically, Jacob was free from disease of the lungs and heart, and with the exception of evidence of syphilitic disease he was in good health.

The report from 27th August described Jacob as being well-behaved since admission. He no longer suffered insomnia, but was now sleeping well and eating food with a keen relish. It's noted that he worked on the farm daily. There was an added comment that there was a nonchalance in his manner which was much unfitted to his condition, and which suggested that he was conscious of a feeling of exaltation.

On 4th September the entry is a lot shorter, stating there was a slight improvement. Jacob was feeling much better, and asking when he could go home. His weight was given at 10st 0lb.

From 10th September through to 16th October there was no change of importance noted. All that changed on 26th October, when it was recorded that Jacob had felt out of sorts for the previous two-three days, and that morning had had an attack of 'giddiness' and faintness that lasted only a few minutes. He was noted as being very depressed, crying for no reason, and had lost his appetite. His heart rate was normal, however his pupils were unequal, the left much larger.

The next entry was dated 8th November, and described how Jacob had had an epileptic-type attack that day. The convulsions were confined almost entirely to the left side. His left pupil was much enlarged.

The report made on 4th December showed that Jacob had also had eczematous eruptions on both thighs, but that it was yielding to medication. There had been no change mentally; he was always bright and lively, and that there had been no despondency since the 8th November entry. His weight was recorded as 9st 3lb.

The last entry from 1890 was on 30th December, and showed the eczemation eruption. He was quite well, and contented with himself and things about him.

The first entry of 1891 was dated 31st January, and it detailed that Jacob had been transferred to No. 4 ward. He still worked on the farm, and was still in the same exalted state.

An entry made on 6th March showed that Jacob was still exalted, and his pupils were markedly unequal. His weight was now 10st 0lb.

5th May reported that he'd had a boil on his neck which was now getting better.

15th July showed a marked difference; he was much worse mentally, and was losing strength and weight. He now needed special feeding, presumably either help feeding himself or a special diet, and it was observed that his pupils were still very unequal in size. His weight was now 8st 7lb.

The next entry was just one week later, on 22nd July. Jacob was now much weaker, and very troublesome. He needed two or three attendants to dress and undress him, and now had to be spoon-fed. The last entry made in his medical journal was on 29th July, and it described Jacob's final hours. At 8.00am on 29th July he suffered an epileptic-style attack; when he was seen at 8.30am his pulse and respiration rates were very rapid and feeble. His pulse was 120 and respiration was 40. There were no physical signs of pulmonary congestion when examined. He had bruises on his left arm and over the end of the sternum, and also over the side of his pelvis caused by a fall.

He thoroughly resisted examination. At 5.00pm his respiration was 40, and moist sounds were noted from the back of both lungs. His pulse couldn't be counted at his wrist, but was noted as 140 at brachial.

At 7.52pm Jacob Levy died and was buried on the grounds of the asylum.

The final record relating to him was made by the coroner, Ernest

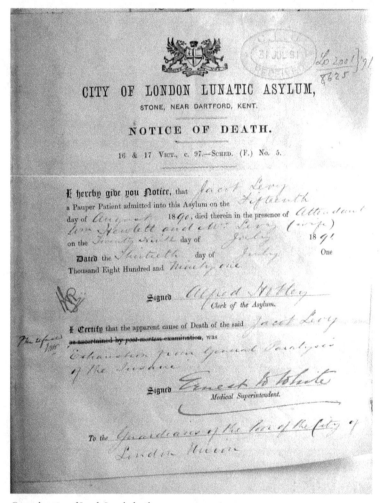

Formal notice of Jacob Levy's death

White. His name was at the top of the entry, dated 30th July 1891. The report showed that Jacob Levy, 35 years old, a butcher of 36 Middlesex Street, Aldgate died at 7.52pm on 29th July 1891. The cause of death was recorded as 'General paralysis of the insane'. He had been in the male infirmary since 29th May last. It was recorded that he had had the disease for the duration of 'some years.'

It was stated clearly that a post-mortem had been refused. Charge attendant Mr Hewlett and Mrs Levy, Jacob's wife, were there at the time of death.

The report was signed by Coroner White, and underneath his signature are the words "Dead 29.Vll.91."

A few months later the Whitechapel murders investigation was scaled back and police officers placed on other crimes.

Newspapers of the time also had theories about who Jack was, and it's interesting to note that Jacob could easily fit into some of the descriptions put forward.

The *London Evening News* of 13th September 1889 reported:

> *The second man is now being watched. He is a resident of the East End, and has been for years. For a long time he has been acting in the most suspicious fashion. He has a business to which he scarcely ever personally attends. He goes about drinking, as is to be met at all hours of the night in the streets all over the neighbourhood. He enters his house at hours when his wife and family have long been at rest. No member of his family dare question him as to his ramblings. He knocks about among the lowest class of women at unearthly hours, although, according to general report, their very appearance is hateful in his sight. His hatred has been produced by physical suffering, for which, like most men of his class, he holds himself perfectly irresponsible. His habits are such as to give one the notion that he is not all together in a fit position to be allowed to roam at will. Whether he has anything to do with the crime, it is, of course, impossible to say, but he is being kept in view.*

The *Rochester Democrat and Chronicle* of 16th September 1889 stated:

JACOB THE RIPPER

The London Police have a theory that "Jack the Ripper" is a crazy Jewish butcher.

On 18th September 1889, in the *North Eastern Daily Gazette*, one detective said in an interview:

> *We are watching now three men, besides the usual night birds of Whitechapel. One man created some stir during the last murders under circumstances which I need not say anything about. He is a curious sort of fellow; in business, but not doing much to keep it going. His wife and daughter see to it, and he is out all hours of the night. He says he is a member of the Vigilance Committee, but I can't answer to that. No, I won't tell you his name, even if you do want to find out if he is a member or not. This man is out all hours of the night, and he lets himself in some [sic] quietly that his wife does not know at what time he really arrives home. She generally finds him in the shop when she comes down in the morning. He is being watched, but we cannot arrest him only on the suspicions we have. We must wait further developments.*

Stone cemetery: could one of these headstones mark the final resting place of Jack the Ripper?

12.

SUMMATION

Why Jacob?

He was Jewish, as police at the time believed the Ripper to be; local to the area, and brought up at the epicentre of the killings. He would have known the warren-like dens of the area like the back of his hand, allowing him to evade capture from the police.

Jacob was a butcher, learning the trade from his father at an early age; the butchering business having been in the family for generations. He grew up in an environment where blood, death and gore were commonplace, possibly even stimulating. This would have given him the necessary skills to slaughter and mutilate quickly and efficiently.

When Jacob was seventeen he discovered the body of his brother hanging from the ceiling. This would obviously have been a traumatic experience that would have stayed with him for the rest of his life, and yet we learn that Jacob later claimed in the asylum records that his brother committed suicide by cutting his own throat. Is it likely, given that this traumatic event would become such an unforgettable incident, that he would confuse the cause of his brother's death? Is it just a coincidence that the way he remembered his brother's suicide was the same cause of death suffered by the victims of Jack the Ripper?

Jacob's life was seemingly going well: a business of his own, a house, married and two children. By 1885 he had moved to 36 Middlesex Street, an address that had been in his family for three generations. Jacob seemed to have his life back on track.

However, it seems he was unable to maintain this level of success and his life took a dramatic about-turn in 1886 when he was arrested for receiving a piece of meat stolen from his neighbour Hyman Sampson.

The day following the arrest his father, Joseph, became ill with an intestinal obstruction, dying eight days later from this along with exhaustion. A common reason for intestinal obstruction is stress and anxiety. It would be understandable that Jacob felt guilty, and perhaps some family members blamed his arrest for the death of his father.

Following his conviction Jacob was sent to Holloway Prison, where he tried to commit suicide and was subsequently placed in an insane asylum. It was there noted that he was depressed, suicidal, restless and violent. These asylum records showed a huge breakdown in his mental health in a short space of time. Jacob's life had come apart.

Could it be that Jacob felt he was in fact innocent of the fencing charge, believing he had been doing if for 'a lark'? What if he felt that he had been set up by Hyman Sampson, who had only just moved his business to Middlesex Street, whereas Jacob's family butchery business had been there for generations? Even if he was guilty, did the punishment fit the crime? Sampson stated he never said he would let Jacob 'off', even if he moved his business. This seems an odd remark to make. What if Sampson had offered exactly that and Jacob refused, expecting to be found Not Guilty or perhaps receive just a slap on the wrist?

Jacob's mental health seemed to improve while in the asylum, and ten months later he was released declared as 'cured', in the February of 1887. His release forms were signed by Godfrey Lushington and Henry Matthews, the Home Secretary.

Once he was released Jacob moved back home to 36 Middlesex Street, where just a few weeks later Hyman Sampson died. This was the man who had him arrested, which in turn could have caused the death his father, which in turn made him try to commit suicide, which in turn had him end up in an asylum. How did the death of Hyman affect Jacob?

Did he feel satisfaction, remorse, or nothing at all?

On 14th October Sarah gave birth to Jacob Levy Jr, 36 weeks and a day after his father had entered the asylum. Obviously it could have just been a premature birth. Research into this shows that an average pregnancy is classed anything from 38 weeks to 42 weeks so it's not impossible, but if Sarah did conceive her son while Jacob was in the asylum this could be the catalyst that caused Jacob's downward spiral.

In May 1888 Jacob's mother died – how did this affect his mental stability?

Jacob was still living at 36 Middlesex Street at this time. This would have enabled him to walk the streets, a man known to everyone – a familiar face in the crowd. It is highly plausible that he could go to all the murder sites and be home within a short period of time, minimising the risk of being seen and caught, but if he was seen the fact he was a butcher and usually awake in the early hours of the morning for markets could easily explain his wanderings, and any possible blood on his clothing.

Jacob was in mental turmoil. He wandered the streets for hours, and didn't sleep at night. He said he felt he would hurt somebody unless he was restrained, and raved that he felt someone was going to do him bodily harm. His mental instability due to the trauma of his brother's suicide and the subsequent depression combined to give Jacob a mental 'deficiency' which hindered him in handling criticism or stress. Added to this, he was now suffering from the effects of what was neurosyphilis, which could very likely have been causing him to have 'episodes' mentally. Physically he would have still been able to behave normally, but his mental capacity would be changing, going through mood-altering phases.

His life was a mess. Then the killings began.

The body of Martha Tabram was found on 7th August 1888, and she had been murdered a short distance away from Jacob's home. Looking at the killings, if you believe Martha to have been a victim of the Ripper and Liz Stride not, a common belief among students of the case, then the pattern of murders can be explained.

A known trait of killers is to kill close to home, in their comfort zone.

Feeling confident after Tabram's murder – he didn't get caught, after all – Jacob moved further afield to Buck's Row, where he murdered Polly Nichols. This time, though, he nearly got caught by a carman. This would have shaken his confidence, so for his next victims he went back to killing closer to home; Middlesex Street is mere minutes away from the murder scenes of Catherine and Mary.

Jacob fits the basic description given by some witnesses: short – a little over five foot in height – aged around thirty and foreign-looking (usually implying Jewish persuasion), although admittedly some may not have seen the victims with the killer.

With regard to the murder of Catherine Eddowes, it was noted at the time in some newspapers that Joseph Hyam Levy, Jacob's cousin, was reluctant to talk about what he had seen. This seems unbelievable, as he was in all likelihood a witness to Catherine Eddowes talking to her murderer. What is noticeable is the discrepancy between the statements of the three men who left the synagogue together that evening. Harry Harris stated he didn't see anything at all, and Joseph Lawende's description was totally different to that of Joseph Hyam Levy, who said he didn't see a lot, only enough to note that the suspect was a few inches taller than Catherine, placing the suspect's height at the same as Jacob's. Was this a subconscious slip, or merely a coincidence?

The fact that it was also believed he knew more than he let on causes us to ask if he saw and recognised his cousin, Jacob. Could it be that on the night in question he believed his cousin was merely consorting with prostitutes? Imagine his horror when the next morning he found out that the same woman had been killed by Jack the Ripper. How would he have felt; could he send his cousin to the gallows by identifying Jacob to the Police? We can only imagine the inner turmoil he must have felt, yet he never once mentioned that he recognised Jacob. We can think of two possible reasons for this.

The first echoes the reason given by Chief Inspector Donald Swanson when writing his well-known marginalia in his retirement: "Because the suspect was also a Jew".

This has always struck us as a strange statement; lots of Jews have testified against fellow Jews. However, would Joseph have testified against a relative, especially given the current climate of anti-semitic feeling? What if Jacob was innocent but the police find him guilty, just like Israel Lipski? What if the press coverage created a frenzy against Jews? Anti-semitic feeling was still high, especially after the Lipski case – would this add more fuel to the fire? What if, instead of identifying his cousin, he decided to keep an eye on him to make sure he didn't attack another woman? Joseph never actually saw Jacob kill Catherine Eddowes – he saw him talking to her, but it is a big step to accepting that his first cousin committed such an atrocious murder.

We know Joseph Hyam Levy was very charitable and a sponsor of immigrants, and it's possible his first thought would be about the Jewish community. Then we have Israel Lipski. We believe that not only did the Jewish population believe Israel Lipski was innocent, they feared the anti-semitic reprisals of the Lipski case.

Jacob is the only suspect for whom the location of Catherine's apron piece and the graffiti can be logically explained by his movements. It's easy to picture Jacob, in a syphilitic rage, murdering and mutilating Catherine Eddowes. Maybe she did indeed suspect him to be the killer and had gone to seek him out, causing his rage and fury at being identified; reason enough to mutilate her with such savagery. Or she could just have been an unfortunate victim at the wrong place at the wrong time. Regardless, we know she was killed and a piece of her apron taken, perhaps to wrap the piece of kidney which the killer had taken with him.

Jacob's route that night is easily imagined. After killing Catherine, it's highly conceivable that he could have left Mitre Square and reached Goulston Street and Wentworth Model Dwellings within a very short period of time.

He had a few options, but the most logical would have been to leave Mitre Square through St James's Passage and on to Duke Street to Houndsditch, and then into Stoney Lane. Here he could have gone home to his butcher's shop, where he could have hidden the kidney with the animal parts. Deciding that he needed to get rid of the apron he would have walked out of his shop, crossed over into New Goulston Street and on to Goulston Street. Walking to the entrance of Wentworth Model Dwellings, he would have then continued through the 'alleyway' to visit his mother's flat, where his sister may still have been residing, or if not then on to his brother's rooms at 214 Wentworth Buildings, staying an hour or so and missing PC Long on his first beat rotation of the area. On leaving, he returned through the back exit, exiting the stairwell at the front of Goulston Street and dropped the apron piece on the way out.

There are alternative options that can be hypothesised with the facts we have put forward as to how the events played out.

Another scenario could be that, after he killed Eddowes, Jacob bypassed home completely and visited his mother's empty rooms to hide the kidney. He then dropped the apron piece in the entrance way, taking his time to write the graffiti using his butcher's chalk, before he visited his sister or brother.

Another alternative could explain Jacob's movements even if there was no rear exit. While walking down from Wentworth Street he may have heard footsteps, perhaps even PC Long on his beat, so hid in the shadows of the entranceway until he passed, deposing of the evidence in the doorway and writing the graffiti.

While the Goulston Street graffiti is in question as being left by Jack the Ripper, we have to ask if it's coincidental that it was placed in the same area that Hyman Sampson had his shop at 58 Goulston Street before he moved to Middlesex Street. It is a shame that the graffiti was never photographed; after all, it could be quite easy to mistake the word 'Juwes' for 'Levys' in the dawn light...

Jacob's asylum records stated that he suffered from syphilis and died from 'paralysis of the insane', the later stages of neurosyphilis. This could explain the killings and why they stopped when they did. Syphilis is a disease that quite often carries a 'timeline', the stages of which Jacob seemed to follow perfectly.

It's likely that he caught syphilis before marrying Sarah, thus being past the contagious stage by the time they married. This would explain how Sarah and their children did not appear to suffer from the illness.

If Sarah had contracted syphilis it would have been probable that they would have lost more children early on in their marriage. This wasn't the case with Sarah. According to the 1911 census record, she reported she had nine children born and seven had survived. It would seem that they lost a child at a very young age, probably between 1883 and 1885, going by the birth dates of the other children.

So if Jacob had caught syphilis before their marriage, he would have gone through stages one and two and be on the latent stage by the time of his marriage. The next stage would be the final stage, and this is where the neurosyphilis advances and exacerbated his mental decline. The average timescale for this was five years. This fits in exactly with Jacob's downward spiral. From fencing the meat in 1886 to his death in 1891, it is exactly five years.

This meant that in 1888 Jacob was most likely dealing with 'episodes', where he would at times be lucid and other times not. Could this have caused him to kill, the illness taking away the safety guard that would stop the urges that drove him? Eventually, however, he would have physically been unable to kill as the illness would take away his coordination and strength.

Looking into Jacob's psyche and the killings themselves, was it coincidence that the Ripper's victims had their throats cut, the exact same method that Jacob remembered as the cause of his brother's suicide? Or that Jack's victims had their intestines ripped out – was it coincidence that Jacob's father died from intestinal problems?

Melville Macnaghten incorrectly stated that 'Kosminski' was placed in a private asylum sometime around March 1889, when in fact he was admitted in July 1890 to the Mile End Workhouse – if we accept Aaron as the Kosminski referred to. Chief Inspector Donald Swanson, in his private marginalia, noted that 'Kosminski' died shortly after his incarceration in Colney Hatch, when Aaron Kosminski – the only inmate of Colney Hatch with that surname – was alive until 1919.

That the suspect died soon after being incarcerated doesn't appear to fit with any known suspect on face value, but we point out that Jacob Levy was placed in an insane asylum and did indeed die a short time later.

If Joseph Hyam Levy was indeed the witness to identify his cousin at the Seaside Home, then perhaps he did so on the condition that the family name of 'Levy' wouldn't be used in records, instead insisting that a pseudonym be used. He had a friend, Martin Kosminski, for whom he assisted in his British naturalization; this man was no relation to Aaron Kosminski, but it was a rare name in London, perhaps used so that it wouldn't be easily confused with anyone else. After all, the police were working under the belief that all this would be kept hushed up in official records and not for the public's eyes. So we have the name 'Kosminski', with no direct link to any man with that name, but we also have the witness Joseph Hyam Levy who had a friend with the same surname – coincidence?

The Lipski case of 1887 had severely damaged Home Secretary Henry Matthews' reputation, the public and press turning against him partly due to his decision to refuse a stay of execution on Israel Lipski. While it was very fortuitous for Matthews that Lipski confessed at the last minute, his image was still tarnished in the public eye. This was due in a large part to W.T. Stead of the *Pall Mall Gazette*, who believed in Lipski's innocence and even likened him to a 'young martyr.' It has always been known that Stead was relentless in his pursuit of justice, and would uphold this 'standard' regardless of the consequences.

All butchers in Whitechapel area were interviewed at the time of the murder. How would Matthews and his career have survived if his 'nemesis' W.T. Stead had found out that a strong suspect for the man terrorising the East End had been released by the Home Secretary the previous year, allowing him to roam the streets murdering and mutilating women?

How would it look to the police and the top echelons of the government if, when interviewing Jacob Levy, it was discovered he had been placed in an insane asylum the previous year and it was the Home Secretary himself who had signed the release papers? What would the public reaction had been if they realised the Home Secretary and the Permanent Under Secretary had released Jack the Ripper onto the streets?

Stead would have whipped up the public until Matthews and possibly even Lushington were hounded from office, an office which in Matthews' case was vital for the Government to stay in power. It would have been enough to realise Lord Salisbury's fears and even topple the British Government.

Robert Sagar was a City of London detective who believed he knew who the suspect was. He stated in a newspaper interview on his retirement that the murderer was a butcher who worked in the vicinity of Butcher's Row in Aldgate High Street, a row of shops that ran along the bottom of Middlesex Street. The suspect stayed at a relative's house, a butcher's shop, and he was partially insane and sent to an asylum. While we don't know if Jacob worked in Butcher's Row, it's not implausible to believe he went there for his meat or even just to visit other butchers. It's also not impossible to believe there was a mistake, and it was by Sagar in Butcher's Row looking up Middlesex Street, where in all likelihood they would have been able to see Joseph Hyam Levy's shop.

Another comment made by Sagar in the newspaper interview was how a police officer had seen a well-dressed Jew exiting Mitre Square a few moments before PC Edward Watkins discovered the body of Catherine Eddowes. Sagar described how officers set off in pursuit of a possible suspect and followed his retreating footsteps as far as King's Block, Artizan Dwellings in Stoney Lane before where they could not hear them anymore. The back of Jacob's shop was practically yards away from King's Block. Is it possible that the reason they lost the suspect was because he simply went home?

◆

Have we proved that Jacob Levy was Jack the Ripper more than 130 years after the fact? No – that would be impossible, but with solid facts and historical data we have proved that he could be linked with almost every aspect of the case, from the locale of the murders and the way in which the victims were slaughtered to the possible psychological reasoning behind each killing.

We've explained why, once Jacob was safely placed in an asylum, the police may have 'mislaid' relevant files, and we've explained why the apron piece and the graffiti were found where they were. We've explained how he easily integrated with the people of the area and the reason for the cessation of the murders.

Finally, we have shown that the descriptions given by some police officers and newspaper reports at the time accumulated to give a description that they believed of a man who lived in the local area, a Jewish butcher who had a business and whose eccentric behaviour left his wife to run that business, and whose rambling and drinking left him at odds with his family. He was also someone who contracted a venereal disease and ended up in an asylum.

Enter Jacob Levy, local Jewish syphilitic butcher... or could we say, Jacob the Ripper?

TIMELINE OF JACOB LEVY

1856	Jacob Levy born
1861	Family live at 111 Middlesex Street
1871	Jacob, aged 15, recorded in census as a butcher
1875	Suicide of Abraham Levy; Jacob discovers the body
1878	Jacob Levy recorded as a butcher of 11 Fieldgate Street
1879	Jacob marries Sarah Abrahams
1879	(17th August) Son Joseph born
1881	(15th January) Son Isaac born
1883	(20th January) Son Lewis born
1883/84	Jacob takes over aunt's butchery business 36 Middlesex Street
1885	Daughter Hannah born
1886	(10th March) Jacob arrested for his involvement in the theft of some meat from neighbour Hyman Sampson
1886	(19th March) Jacob's father died
1886	(5th April) Found Guilty at the Old Bailey and sentenced to 12 months' with hard labour. Sent to Holloway Prison
1886	(19th April) Transferred to Chelmsford Prison
1886	(21st May) Certified insane and subsequently admitted to Essex Insane Asylum

1886   (8th June) Son Nathan born
1887   (3rd February) Released and returns to 36 Middlesex Street
1887   (2nd April) Death of Hyman Sampson
1887   (14th October) Son Jacob Jr born
1888   (18th May) Jacob's mother died
1889   Daughter Caroline born
1890   (18th July) Son Moss born
1890   (14th August) Jacob admitted to Stone House Hospital
1891   (22nd July) Jacob Levy died

LEVY GENEALOGY

Joseph Levy
Jacob Levy's father.

Born   1821 (JewishGen.org)
Married   1848 (3rd September) (Synagogue scribes)
Died   1886 (19th March) (Death certificate)
Father Isaac Levy (Yitzak) (Synagogue scribes)
Mother   Sarah (JewishGen.org)
Spouse   Caroline Solomons (Synagogue scribes)
Children   Rebecca Solomons (stepdaughter) 1836 (Ancestry)
            Jane Solomons (stepdaughter) 1841 (Birth certificate)
            Hannah Levy 1847 (14th September) (Birth certificate)
            Elizabeth 1848 (Ancestry)
            Sarah 1851 (8th July) (JewishGen.org)
            Isaac 1852 (Ancestry)
            Abraham 1854 (Ancestry)
            Jacob 1856 (Birth certificate)
            Moss/Moses 1859 (Ancestry)
            Rebecca 1867 (June) (JewishGen.org)

Timeline

1821 Born (Ancestry)

1841 38 Petticoat Lane (1841 census)

1847 (14th September) Birth of Hannah (Birth certificate)

1847 (14th September) 5 Love Court (Birth certificate)

1848 (3rd September) Married Caroline (Marriage certificate)

1848 (3rd September) 4 Little Middlesex Street (Marriage certificate)

1848 Birth of Elizabeth (1851 census)

1851 (8th July) Birth of Sarah (JewishGen.org)

1851 4 Little Middlesex Street (1851 census)

1852 5 Swan Court (Insurance policy)

1852 Birth of Isaac (1861 census)

1854 Birth of Abraham (1861 census)

1854 111 Middlesex Street (Insurance policy)

1856 (11th March) Birth of Jacob (Birth certificate)

1856 (11th March) 111 Middlesex Street (Birth certificate)

1859 Birth of Moss (1861 census)

1861 111 Middlesex Street (1861 census)

1865 111 Middlesex Street (Post Office Directory, London)

1866 111 Middlesex Street (Post Office Directory, London)

1867 (June) Birth of Rebecca (Jewish Free Schools)

1868 111 Middlesex Street (*Jewish Chronicle*)

1871 111 Middlesex Street (1871 census)

1875 (19th May) Suicide of Abraham (Newspaper report)

1875 (19th May) 111 Middlesex Street (Newspaper report)

1878 111 Middlesex Street (*Jewish Chronicle*)

1880 111 Middlesex Street (*Jewish Chronicle*)

1881 7 Globe Road (1881 census)

1886 (10th March) Arrest of Jacob (Old Bailey records)

1886 (19th March) Died (Death certificate)

1886 (19th March) 28 Goulston Street (Death certificate)

Notes

Synagogue Scribes Ref GSMa 082/72
Family Name: Levy & Solomons
Forename: Joseph & Catherine
Hebrew name: Joseph / Brynah

Event: Marriage Date 1848 [3rd September] Father's Hebrew name –
  Isaac / Isaac
Spouse: Solomons Catherine / Levy Joseph
By whom registered: Simon Oppenheim
Day of marriage: 3rd September 1848
Name of witness: [Hebrew]
By whom married: [Hebrew]
Bride's name: Catherine Solomons
Bridegroom's name: [Hebrew] Joseph Levy [no.] 72 LDS microfilm
  (brief) 1791-1865, 2nd Vol pg 82. 1848 Great Synagogue Chambers
Parish of St James, Duke's Place, City of London IG. Third day of
September 1848

Name: Joseph Levy / Catherine Solomons
Age: Full / Full
Status: Bachelor / Widow
Occupation: Butcher
Address: 4 Little Middlesex Street / 4 Little Middlesex Street
Father's name: Isaac Levy / Abraham Solomons
Father's occupation: Deceased / Deceased

Great Synagogue Jewish Religion [signature]
Joseph Levy [Signature] / X the mark of Catherine Solomons
Mark Marks / Hyam Jonas [both common witnesses]
Simon Oppenheim, Secretary of the Great Synagogue Duke's Place

LDS film 94661 marriage register printed film) pg10 marriage September
1848, Catherine Solomons, Joseph Levy, St Luke's 2 288

Insurance Policy
L1026_1 Joseph Levy, Gent, 5 Swan Court, Middlesex Street 653-
  08.04.1852-1674364
L1026_2 Joseph Levy, butcher, 111 Middlesex Street 136-p72-
  06.02.1854-167436 [We've added the Swan Court address as it looks like
these addresses have been insured by the same person given the identical
docket number and end policy number.]

Misc
Joseph was listed in the *Jewish Chronicle* in 1868 as an authorised Kosher
butcher. He died on 19th May 1886 aged 66 of intestinal obstruction and
exhaustion.

Caroline/Catherine Levy

Jewish Name: Brynah. Jacob Levy's mother.

Born 1819 (Ancestry)
Married Groom [unknown?]
1848 (Marriage certificate)
Died 1888 (18th May) (Death certificate)
Father Abraham Solomons (Marriage certificate)
Spouse Joshua Solomons 1846 (22nd March) (Death certificate)
Joseph Levy (Marriage certificate)
Children Rebecca Solomons 1836 (Ancestry)
Jane Solomons 1841 (10th November) (Birth certificate)
Elizabeth 1847 (Birth certificate)
Hannah 1848 (14th September) (Ancestry)
Sarah 1851 (8th July) (JewishGen.org)
Isaac 1852 (Ancestry)
Abraham 1854 (Ancestry)
Jacob 1856 (11th March) (Birth certificate)
Moss/Moses 1859 (Ancestry)
Rebecca 1867 (June) (JewishGen.org)

Timeline

1819 Born (Ancestry)
1836 Birth of Rebecca (Ancestry)
1839 (10th November) Birth of Jane (Birth certificate)
1839 (10th November) 9 Freeman Street (Birth certificate)
1846 (22nd March) Death of Joshua (Death certificate)
1846 (22nd March) 5 Love Court (Death certificate)
1847 (14th September) Birth of Hannah (Birth certificate)
1847 (14th September) 5 Love Court (Birth certificate)
1848 (3rd September) Marriage to Joseph (Marriage certificate)
1848 (3rd September) 4 Little Middlesex Street (Marriage certificate)
1848 Birth of Elizabeth (1851 census)
1851 4 Little Middlesex Street (1851 census)
1851 (8th July) Birth of Sarah (JewishGen.org)
1852 5 Swan Court (JewishGen.org)
1852 Birth of Isaac (1861 census)
1854 Birth of Abraham (1861 census)

1856 (11th March) Birth of Jacob (Birth certificate)
1856 (11th March) 111 Middlesex Street (Birth certificate)
1859 Birth of Moss/Moses (1861 census)
1861 111 Middlesex Street (1861 census)
1865 111 Middlesex Street *(Jewish Chronicle)*
1866 111 Middlesex Street *(Jewish Chronicle)*
1867 (June) Birth of Rebecca Levy (Jewish Free Schools)
1868 111 Middlesex Street *(Jewish Chronicle)*
1871 111 Middlesex Street (1871 census)
1878 111 Middlesex Street *(Jewish Chronicle)*
1880 111 Middlesex Street *(Jewish Chronicle)*
1881 7 Globe Road (1881 census)
1875 (19th May) Suicide of Abraham (Newspaper report)
1875 (19th May) 111 Middlesex Street (Newspaper report)
1878 111 Middlesex Street *(Jewish Chronicle)*
1886 (10th March) Arrest of Jacob (Old Bailey records)
1886 (19th March) Death of Joseph (Death certificate)
1886 (19th March) 28 Goulston Street (Death certificate)
1888 (18th May) Died (Death certificate)
1888 (18th May) 198 Wentworth buildings (Death certificate)

Notes

Joshua Solomons, Caroline's first husband, died on 22nd March 1846 aged 31 at 5 Love Court of phthisis. He was buried on 23rd March 1846 at Brady Street Cemetery. Going by Jewish tradition we believe that 'Rebecca' was an important name to Caroline, the eldest and youngest child being named it. Could this be a family member – perhaps her mother? We think 'Jane' was probably from Joshua's side, as nobody in the Levy side follows this name.

1848 Great Synagogue Chambers, City of London, has a wedding certificate listing Catherine's father as Abraham Solomons; he was dead in 1848.

Rebecca Solomons
Jewish name Rebkah. Jacob Levy's half-sister.

Born   1836 (Ancestry)
Married   1856 (6th May) (Synagogue scribes)
Died   1908 (Ancestry)
Father   Joshua Solomons (Husband's inquest report)

Mother   Caroline Solomons (Ancestry)
Spouse   Nathan Hyams (Synagogue scribes)
Children   Caroline 1856 (Ancestry)
            Joseph 1858 (Ancestry)
            Emanuel 1866 (31st March) (JewishGen.org)
            Julia 1869 (22 August) (JewishGen.org)
            Miriam/Mary 1871 (4th September) (JewishGen.org)
            Phoebe [Nykerk] 1876 (30th October) (Ancestry)
            Caroline 1879 (Ancestry)

Timeline

1836 Born (Ancestry)
1846 (22nd March) Death of father Joshua Solomons (Death certificate)
1846 (22nd March) 5 Love Court (Death certificate)
1851 4 Little Middlesex Street (1851 census)
1856 (6th May) Marriage to Nathan Hyams (Marriage certificate)
1856 (6th May) 111 Middlesex Street (Marriage certificate)
1856 Birth of Caroline (1861 census)
1858 Birth of Joseph (1861 census)
1861 136 Wentworth Street (1861 census)
1866 (31st March) Birth of Emanuel (Jewish Free Schools)
1869 (22nd August) Birth of Julia (Jewish Free Schools)
1871 136 Wentworth Street (1871 census)
1871 (4th September) Birth of Mary (Jewish Free Schools)
1874 36 Wentworth Street (Jewish Free Schools)
1876 (30th October) Birth of Phoebe (1939 Register)
1878 136 Wentworth Street (Jewish Free Schools)
1879 Birth of Caroline (1881 census)
1881 123 Middlesex Street (1881 census)
1881 Also noted at 217 Mile End Road (1881 census)
1883 (19th October) Suicide of Nathan Hyams (JewishGen.org)
1891 14 Foley Street (1891 census)
1901 52 Brushfield Street (1901 census)
1908 Death (Ancestry)

Notes

A few inconsistencies here. The 1881 census has the family in two places.
They are recorded at 123 Middlesex Street and also 217 Mile End Road.

The Nathan of 123 Middlesex Street was a fishmonger, and Nathan of 217 Mile End Road was a wet/dry fishmonger. The 217 Mile End address has the Jewish version of Rebecca's name. Finally, the 217 address has Caroline, aged two, living there, whereas there is no mention of her at 123 Middlesex Street. We do know there was a Caroline born at that time. This could be a huge coincidence and these are two different families, or could it be one is a place of work and the other the family's residence? The JFS record has the family living at 36 Wentworth Street in 1874. This is probably a transcription error and should be 136.

Nathan Hyams

Rebecca Solomons's husband.

Born	1835 (Ancestry)
Married	1856 (6th May) (Synagogue scribes)
Died	1883 (JewishGen.org)
Father	Joseph Mitchell Hyams (JewishGen.org)
Mother	Julia Joel (JewishGen.org)
Spouse	Rebecca Solomons (Synagogue scribes)
Children	Caroline 1856 (Ancestry)
	Joseph 1858 (Ancestry)
	Emanuel 1866 (31st March) (JewishGen.org)
	Julia [Cohen] 1869 (22nd August) (JewishGen.org)
	Miriam/Mary 1871 (4th September) (JewishGen.org)
	Phoebe [Nykerk] 1876 (30th October) (Ancestry)
	Caroline 1879 (Ancestry)
Siblings	Leah 1833 (Ancestry)
	Nathan 1836 (Ancestry)
	John/Jack/Jacob 1837 (JewishGen.org)
	Abraham 1838 (Ancestry)
	Daniel 1841 (JewishGen.org)
	Rose/Rosa 1843 (JewishGen.org)
	Rebecca 1845 (JewishGen.org)
	Hyam 1850 (JewishGen.org)
	Amelia 1852 (Ancestry)
	Sarah 1855 (Ancestry)
	Caroline 1859 (Ancestry)

JACOB THE RIPPER

Timeline

1835 Born (Ancestry)

1841 3 Tuns Alley (1841 census)

1851 107 Middlesex Street (1851 census)

1856 (6th May) Marriage to Rebecca Solomons (Marriage certificate)

1856 (6th May) 107 Middlesex Street (Marriage certificate)

1856 Birth of Caroline (1861 census)

1858 Birth of Joseph Mitchell (1861 census)

1861 136 Wentworth Street (1861 census)

1866 (31st March) Birth of Emanuel (Jewish Free Schools)

1869 (22nd August) Birth of Julia (Jewish Free Schools)

1871 136 Wentworth Street (1871 census)

1871 (4th September) Birth of Mary (Jewish Free Schools)

1874 36 Wentworth Street (Jewish Free Schools)

1876 (30th October) Birth of Phoebe (1939 Register)

1878 136 Wentworth Street (Jewish Free Schools)

1879 Birth of Caroline (1881 census)

1881 123 Middlesex Street (1881 census)

1881 also noted at 217 Mile End Road (1881 census)

1883 (19th October) Died (JewishGen.org)

Notes

Jewish Chronicle, 26th October 1883:

Sad death – On Tuesday the City Coroner, Mr Payne, held an inquest at the Coroner's Court, Golden Lane on the body of Nathan Hyams, aged 49, a fishmonger, lately dwelling in Sandy's Row, Bishopsgate. Deceased, it appeared, had been very unfortunate in business, and was in such reduced circumstances that he could scarcely maintain himself and family. They had suffered a great deal of privation, and their condition preyed very much upon the deceased's mind. On Friday morning last, his son found him hanging by the neck by a rope, which was fastened to the banisters of the stairs. Medical evidence was given that death resulted from strangulation, and the jury returned a verdict to the effect that the deceased committed suicide whilst of unsound mind.

Jane Solomons/Levy

Jacob Levy's half-sister.

Born   1839 (10th November) (Birth certificate)
Father   Joshua Solomons (Birth certificate)
Mother   Caroline Solomons (Birth certificate)

Timeline

1839   (10th November) Birth (Birth certificate)
1839   (10th November) 9 Freeman Street (Birth certificate)
1851   4 Little Middlesex Street (1851 census)
1861   111 Middlesex Street (1861 census)

Notes

Her father Joshua Solomons was noted as John on the birth certificate. In the 1851 census Jane is recorded as Jane Levy, wife's daughter, however in the 1861 census she is back to the name Jane Solomons.

Hannah Levy

Jacob Levy's sister.

Born   1847 (14 September) (Birth certificate)
Married   1868 (Q2) (Ancestry)
Died   1881 (Q2) (Ancestry)
Father   Joseph Levy (Birth certificate)
Mother   Caroline Solomons (Birth certificate)
Spouse   Henry Cohen (Ancestry)
Children   Esther 1869 (Ancestry)
            Emanuel 1870 (7th October) (Jewish Free Schools)
            Isaac 1872 (3rd September) (Jewish Free Schools)
            Joseph 1874 (15th May) (Ancestry)
            Abraham 1875 (Ancestry)
            Esther 1879 (Ancestry)

Timeline

1847   (14th September) Born (Birth certificate)
1847   (14th September) 5 Love Court (Birth certificate)
1851   4 Little Middlesex Street (1851 census)
1861   111 Middlesex Street (1861 census)

1868   (1st March) Marriage to Henry Cohen (Marriage certificate)
1868   (1st March) 111 Middlesex Street (Marriage certificate)
1869   Birth of Esther (1871 census)
1870   (7th October) Birth of Emanuel (Jewish Free Schools)
1871   6 Horseshoe Court (1871 census)
1872   (3rd April) Death of Esther (Death certificate)
1872   (3rd April) 6 Horseshoe Place (Death certificate)
1872   (3rd September) Birth of Isaac (Jewish Free Schools)
1874   (15th May) Birth of Joseph (School record)
1875   Birth of Abraham (1881 census)
1878   6 Horseshoe Place (Jewish Free Schools)
1879   Birth of Esther (1891 census)
1880   6 Horseshoe Place (Jewish Free Schools)
1881   6 Horseshoe Place (1881 census)
1881   (8th April) Died (Death certificate)
1881   (8th April) 6 Horseshoe Place (Death certificate)

Notes

Hannah died on 8th April 1881, aged 33, from pulmonary phthisis.

Their daughter Esther died 3rd April 1872 from pertussis (whooping cough) aged 4. Joseph Levy of 111 Middlesex Street was the informant of the death – Joseph was her grandfather.

Esther Cohen (younger sister to Esther who died in 1872) was born in 1879 and was at the residence of her uncle (Henry's brother Isaac) in the 1881 census.

The school record of Emmanuel has his date of birth as 7th October 1890. This we feel is a mistake, as he was admitted to the school on 14th March. We believe this is a transcription error, and should have been 7th October 1870.

Henry Cohen
Hannah Levy's husband.

Born   1847 (Ancestry)
Married   1868 (1st March) (Marriage certificate)
Died   1881 (Q2) (Ancestry)
Father   Emanuel Cohen (Marriage certificate)

Mother	Esther Abrahams (Synagogue scribes)
Spouse	Hannah Levy (Marriage certificate)
	Louisa Elizabeth Jackson (Ancestry)
Children	Esther 1869 (Ancestry)
	Emanuel 1870 (7th October) (Jewish Free Schools)
	Francis 1871 (Ancestry)
	Isaac 1872 (3rd September) (Jewish Free Schools)
	Joseph 1874 (15th May) (Ancestry)
	Abraham 1875 Census
	Esther 1879 (Ancestry)
Siblings	Samuel 1847 (Ancestry)
	Benjamin 1849 (Ancestry)
	Deborah 1851 (Ancestry)
	Isaac 1854 (Ancestry)
	John 1855 (Ancestry)
	Aaron 1856 (Ancestry)
	Rachel 1858 (Ancestry)
	Abraham 1860 (Ancestry)
	Edward 1864 (Ancestry)
	Esther 1865 (Ancestry)

Timeline

1846 Born (Ancestry)
1851 20 Butler Street (1851 census)
1868 (1st March) Marriage to Hannah Levy (Marriage certificate)
1868 (1st March) 111 Middlesex Street (Marriage certificate)
1869 Birth of Esther (1871 census)
1870 (7th October) Birth of Emanuel (Jewish Free Schools)
1871 6 Horseshoe Court (1871 census)
1872 (3rd April) Death of Esther (Death certificate)
1872 (3rd April) 6 Horseshoe Place (Death certificate)
1872 (3rd September) Birth of Isaac (Jewish Free Schools)
1874 (15th May) Birth of Joseph (School record)
1875 Birth of Abraham (1881 census)
1878 6 Horseshoe Place (Jewish Free Schools)
1879 Birth of Esther (1891 census)
1880 6 Horseshoe Place (Jewish Free Schools)
1881 6 Horseshoe Place (1881 census)

1881 (8th April) Death of Hannah (Death certificate)
1881 (8th April) 6 Horseshoe Place (Death certificate)
1883 63 Norfolk Buildings (School record)
1891 5 Pauline Terrace (1891 census)
1891 (Q4) Marriage to Louisa (Ancestry)
1892 Birth of Edward (Ancestry)
1893 (12th July) Birth of Deborah (School record)
1894 (22nd October) Birth of Louisa (School record)
1896 Birth of Henry (1901 census)
1894 (15th January) Birth of Irene (School record)
1898 (1st June) 4 Norwich Road (School record)
1901 Birth of Benjamin (1901 census)
1904 (19th January) 4 Norwich Road (School record)
1911 4 Norwich Road (1911 census)
1924 Death (Ancestry)

Notes

While just an assumption on our part, we feel it's highly unlikely given the names etc that Henry's second wife Louisa was Jewish. She was noted as a lunatic in Epsom asylum in the 1911 census.

Elizabeth Levy

Jacob Levy's sister.

Born   1849 (Ancestry)
Married   1873 (Q4) (Birth, Marriage Death website)
Died   1910 (3rd July) (Ancestry)
Father   Joseph Levy (JewishGen.org)
Mother   Caroline Solomons (JewishGen.org)
Spouse   Isaac Barnett (Ancestry)
Children   Samuel 1877 (24th August) (JewishGen.org)
           Emanuel 1879 (Q3) (Birth, Marriage Death website)
           Hannah 1881 (Q3) (Birth, Marriage Death website)
           Moses Judah 1883 (23rd January) (Ancestry)
           Abraham Alfred 1884 (Q2) (Birth, Marriage Death website)
           Phoebe 1886 (6th February) (Ancestry)
           Caroline 1889 (14th June) (Ancestry)

Timeline

1847 Born (1851 census)
1851 4 Little Middlesex Street (1851 census)
1861 111 Middlesex Street (1861 census)
1871 111 Middlesex Street (1871 census)
1873 (Q4) Marriage to Isaac Barnett (Birth, Marriage Death website)
1876 (24th August) Birth of Samuel (Jewish Free Schools)
1879 (Q3) Birth of Emmanuel (1881 census)
1881 48 Middlesex Street (1881 census)
1881 (Q3) Birth of Hannah (1881 census)
1883 (23rd January) Birth of Moses Judah (1939 Register)
1883 48 Petticoat Lane (Jewish Free Schools)
1884 (Q2) Birth of Abraham (1891 census)
1886 (6th February) birth of Phoebe (1939 Register)
1889 (14th June) birth of Caroline (1939 Register)
1891 87 Middlesex Street (1891 census)
1901 18 Newsham Street (1901 census)
1908 (3rd July) Died (*Jewish Chronicle*)

Notes

Jewish Chronicle, 7th June 1909:

Barnett/Drukker: On the 7th June at Bonn's Hotel Great Prescott Street by the Rev M Hart. Emanuel, son of Mr and Mrs Isaac Barnett of 16 Grafton Street Mile End to Julia, daughter of Mr and Mrs Drukker 85 Middlesex Street E.

Isaac Barnett

Elizabeth Levy's husband.

Born	1848 (Ancestry)
Married	1873 (Q4) (Ancestry)
Died	1918 (Ancestry)
Father	Samuel Barnett (Ancestry)
Mother	Phoebe Judah (Ancestry)
Spouse	Elizabeth Levy (Ancestry)
Children	Samuel 1877 (24th August) (JewishGen.org)
	Emanuel 1879 (Q3) (Birth, Marriage Death website)

Hannah 1881 (Q3) (Birth, Marriage Death website)
Moses Judah 1883 (23rd January) (Ancestry)
Abraham Alfred 1884 (Q2) (Birth, Marriage Death website)
Phoebe 1886 (6th February) (Ancestry)
Caroline 1889 (14th June) (Ancestry)

Siblings Sarah 1854 (Ancestry)
Samuel 1856 (Ancestry)
Rachael 1858 (Ancestry)
Henry 1859 (Ancestry)
Moses 1862 (Ancestry)

Timeline

1848 Born (1861 census)
1861 49 Petticoat Lane (1861 census)
1871 49 Petticoat Lane (1871 census)
1873 (Q4) Marriage to Elizabeth Levy (Birth, Marriage Death)
1876 (24th August) Birth of Samuel (Jewish Free Schools)
1879 Birth of Emmanuel (1881 census)
1881 48 Middlesex Street (1881 census)
1881 Birth of Hannah (1891 census)
1883 (23rd January) Birth of Moses (1939 Register)
1883 48 Petticoat Lane (Jewish Free Schools)
1884 Birth of Abraham (1891 census)
1886 (6th February) Birth of Phoebe (1939 Register)
1889 (14th June) Birth of Caroline (1939 Register)
1891 87 Middlesex Street (1891 census)
1901 18 Newsham Stepney (1901 census)
1908 (3rd July) death of Elizabeth (JewishGen.org)
1911 25 Wesbaden Road (1911 census)
1918 Died (Ancestry)

Notes

Jewish Chronicle, 28th March 1890:

AN UNDOUBTED SUCCESS

I. Barnett

Wishes to inform the Jewish Community that he will have on show of the
FINEST CHEDDAR AND DUTCH CHEESE for the ensuing holiday to be

obtained.

I.B cautions intending purchasers against buying spurious imitations of kosher cheddar cheese, he being the only maker in England licensed by the Ecclestical Authorities and made under direct supervision.

87 Middlesex Street

Sarah Levy

Jacob Levy's sister.

Born	1851 (8th July) (JewishGen.org)
Father	Joseph Levy (Ancestry)
Mother	Caroline Solomons (Ancestry)

Timeline

1851   4 Little Middlesex Street (1851 census)

Notes

We have no further information on Sarah, so it's likely that she died before the 1861 census.

Isaac Levy

Jacob Levy's brother.

Born	1853 (Birth, Marriage Death website)
Married	1873 (23rd March) (Ancestry)
Died	1901 (Ancestry)
Father	Joseph Levy (Ancestry)
Mother	Caroline Solomons (Ancestry)
Spouse	Clara Marks (Ancestry)
Children	Miriam [Smith] 1873 (Ancestry)
	Abraham 1875 (Ancestry)
	Caroline/Catherine [Abrahams] 1876 (25th March) (Ancestry)
	Sarah 1878 (Ancestry)
	Hannah 1880 (Ancestry)
	Elizabeth [Marinofski] 1882 (19th June) (Ancestry)
	Woolf 1884 (Ancestry)
	Joseph 1887 (Ancestry)

Rebecca 1888 (Ancestry)
Moses 1891 (Ancestry)
Leah [Barth] 1893 (15th July) (Ancestry)

Timeline

1853   Born (Birth, Marriage Death website)
1861   111 Middlesex Street (1861 census)
1871   111 Middlesex Street (1871 census)
1873   (23rd March) Marriage to Clara Marks (Ancestry)
1873   Birth of Miriam (1881 census)
1875   Birth of Abraham (1881 census)
1876   (25th March) Birth of Caroline/Catherine (1939 Register)
1878   Birth of Sarah (1881 census)
1880   Birth of Hannah (1881 census)
1881   71 Ernest Street (1881 census)
1882   (19th June) Birth of Elizabeth (1939 Register)
1884   Birth of Woolf (1891 census)
1887   Birth of Joseph (1891 census)
1888   (23rd November) Birth of Rebecca (1891 census)
1888   (23rd November) 214 Wentworth Buildings (Ancestry)
1891   130 Wentworth Buildings (1891 census)
1891   Birth of Moss (1901 census)
1893   (15th July) Birth of Leah (1939 Register)
1901   130 Wentworth Buildings (1901 census)
1901   Died (Ancestry)

Notes

Isaac died from tuberculosis and exhaustion at 130 Wentworth Buildings in 1901.

Clara Marks

Isaac Levy's wife.

Born   (Q1) 1853 (Birth, Marriage Death website)
Married   1873 (22nd March) (Ancestry)
Died   1929 (Ancestry)
Father   Woolf Marks (Synagogue scribes)
Mother   Mary Simmons (Synagogue scribes)

Spouse	Isaac Levy (Ancestry)
Children	Miriam [Smith] 1873 (Ancestry)
	Abraham 1875 (Ancestry)
	Caroline/Catherine[Abrahams] 1876 (25th March) (Ancestry)
	Sarah 1878 (Ancestry)
	Hannah 1880 (Ancestry)
	Elizabeth [Marinofski] 1882 (10th June) (Ancestry)
	Woolf 1884 (Ancestry)
	Joseph 1887 (Ancestry)
	Rebecca 1888 (Ancestry)
	Moses 1891 (Ancestry)
	Leah [Barth] 1893 (15th July) (Ancestry)
Siblings	Jacob 1837 (Ancestry)
	Jane 1840 (Ancestry)
	Aaron 1844 (Ancestry)
	Joshua 1847 (Ancestry)
	Henry 1849 (Ancestry)
	Hannah 1854 (Ancestry)
	Woolf 1856 (Ancestry)
	Besty 1858 (Ancestry)

Timeline

1853 Born (Birth, Marriage Death website)
1861 11 Fire Ball Court (1861 census)
1871 257 Old Kent Road (1871 census)
1873 (23rd March) Marriage to Isaac Levy (Ancestry)
1873 Birth of Miriam (1881 census)
1875 Birth of Abraham (1881 census)
1876 (25th March) Birth of Caroline/Catherine (1939 Register)
1878 Birth of Sarah (1881 census)
1880 Birth of Hannah (1881 census)
1881 71 Ernest Street (1881 census)
1882 (19th June) Birth of Elizabeth (1939 Register)
1884 Birth of Woolf (1891 census)
1887 Birth of Joseph (1891 census)
1888 (23rd November) Birth of Rebecca (1891 census)
1888 (23rd November) 214 Wentworth Buildings (Ancestry)

1891   130 Wentworth Buildings (1891 census)
1891   Birth of Moss (1901 census)
1893   (15th July) Birth of Leah (1939 Register)
1901   130 Wentworth Buildings (1901 census)
1901   Death of Isaac (Ancestry)
1911   10 Lichfield Road Bow (1911 census)
1929   (15th October) Died (Ancestry)

Abraham Levy

Jacob Levy's brother.

Born	1854 (Ancestry)
Died	1875 (19th May) (Newspaper report)
Father	Joseph Levy (Newspaper report)
Mother	Caroline Solomons (Ancestry)

Timeline

1854   (Q3) Born (Birth, Marriage Death website)
1861   111 Middlesex Street (1861 census)
1871   111 Middlesex Street (1871 census)
1875   (19th May) Death (Newspaper report)
1875   (19th May) 111 Middlesex Street (Newspaper report)

Notes

Abraham committed suicide at 111 Middlesex Street on 19th May 1875.

ABRAHAM LEVY

The tombstone to the memory of ABRAHAM LEVY, son of JOSEPH LEVY, Butcher, of 111 Middlesex Street, Whitechapel, will be set 15 August, 1875 at West Ham.

Moses Levy

Jacob Levy's brother.

Born	Q3 1859 (Birth, Marriage Death website)
Father	Joseph Levy (Ancestry)
Mother	Caroline (Ancestry)

Timeline

1859 (Q3) Born (Birth, Marriage Death website)
1861 111 Middlesex Street (1861 census)
1871 111 Middlesex Street (1871 census)

Rebecca Levy

Jacob Levy's sister.

Born   1867 (Jewish Free Schools)
Father   Joseph Levy (Jewish Free Schools)
Mother   Caroline Solomons (Ancestry)

Timeline

1867 (Q2) Born (Jewish Free Schools)
1875 Admitted to school (Jewish Free Schools)
1875 111 Middlesex Street (Jewish Free Schools)
1881 7 Globe Road (1881 census)

Notes

Jews Free School

Daughter – Rebecca Born 6/1867
Admitted – 01/05/1875 Number 8873
Father – Joseph Levy, Address 111 Middlesex Street
Reason left – 05/1875 Infant school

A few inconsistencies here. There is no record of her birth in BMD or Ancestry. We literally have to go with the Jewish Free School records. Either Rebecca wasn't her legal name, her birth wasn't registered, or it has been lost over the years.

We have no record of her anywhere in the 1871 census. She should be there aged 4.

* * *

FAMILY OF JOSEPH HYAM LEVY

Hyam Levy

Jewish Name Chaim, b. Isaac AKA Haim Levy, Hyam Levi, Hayim

Levy. Joseph Hyam Levy's father.

Born	1810 (Synagogue scribes)
Married	1834 (31st December) (Synagogue scribes)
Died	1872 (25th November) (Ancestry)
Father	Isaac Levy (Synagogue scribes)
Mother	Sarah (Synagogue scribes)
Spouse	Frances Naphtali (Synagogue scribes)
Children	Isaac 1836 (Ancestry)
	Naphtali 1838 (Ancestry)
	Sarah 1840 (Ancestry)
	Joseph Hyam 1842 (Ancestry)
	Rachael 1843 (JewishGen.org)
	Mordecai 1845 (JewishGen.org)
	Elias 1848 (Ancestry)
	Henry 1850 (Ancestry)
	Elizabeth 1855 (Ancestry)
Siblings	Esther [Lyons/Simmons] 1812 (Ancestry)
	Elias 1816 (Ancestry)
	Moss 1818 (Ancestry)
	Joseph 1821 (Ancestry)
	Elizabeth 1826 (Ancestry)

Timeline

1810 (29th April) Born (Synagogue scribes)
1810 Petticoat Lane (Synagogue scribes)
1822 36 Petticoat Lane (*Underhill's Directory*)
1834 (31st December) Marriage to Frances (Synagogue scribes)
1835 (23rd October) 41½ Petticoat Lane (Insurance policy)
1836 Birth of Isaac (1841 census)
1836 42 Petticoat Lane Pigot
1836 (21st April) 41½ Petticoat Lane (Freedom of the City)
1838 Birth of Naphtali (1841 census)
1839 36 Petticoat Lane (*Pigot's Directory*)
1840 36 Middlesex Street (*Pigot's Directory*)
1840 Birth of Sarah (1841 census)
1841 36 Petticoat Lane (1841 census)
1841 Birth of Joseph Hyam (1851 census)

1843   Birth of Rachael (JewishGen.org)
1845   Birth of Mordecai (JewishGen.org)
1846   (18th February) 36 Middlesex Street (Insurance policy)
1848   Birth of Elias (1851 census)
1849   36 Petticoat Lane (1849 *Post Office Directory*)
1850   Birth of Henry (1851 census)
1851   36 Petticoat Lane (1851 census)
1852   6 Middlesex Street (Insurance policy)
1852   (8th July) 36 Middlesex Street (Insurance policy)
1855   Birth of Elizabeth (1861 census)
1861   36 Petticoat Lane (1861 census)
1865   36 Middlesex Street (Post Office Directory, London)
1866   36 Middlesex Street (Post Office Directory, London)
1868   (13th November) 36 Middlesex Street (*Jewish Chronicle* Kosher record)
1871   36 Petticoat Lane (1871 census)
1872   (25 November) Died (Probate)

Notes

Birth rec Synagogue Scribes
Ref GSB L038
Name – Levy
Hebrew Name – [blank]
Event – Birth
Date – 1810 (April – May)
Address – Petticoat Lane
Father – Isaac
Father's Hebrew name – Isaac Isaac b Hayim
Mother's family name – [blank]
Mother's name – Sarah
Mother's Hebrew name – Sarah

Synagogue scribes – GSM 301/10 Marriage records
Family name – Levy Napthali
Forename – Hyam Frances
Hebrew name – Chaim Brynah
Event – Marriage Marriage
Date – 1834 [31st December] 1834 [31st December]

Occupation – [blank] [blank]
Address – [blank] [blank]
Father's name – [blank] Joseph
Father's Hebrew name – Isaac [blank]
Mother's Hebrew name – [blank] [blank]
Spouse – Naphtali Frances Levy Hyam

Freedom of the City 21 April 1836
Hyam Levy

I, Hyam Levy of the age 26 years (son of Isaac Levy, late of Petticoat Lane, butcher deceased) occupying premises in No 41½ Petticoat Lane in the Parish of St Botolph, Aldgate in the Ward of Portsoken and carrying on the business of butcher, do hereby apply to be admitted to the Freedom of The City of London by redemption on pursuance of the Resolution of the Court of Common Council of the 17th and 19th March 1835.

[Handwritten notes underneath state Jewish persuasion, British born, Father British born]

[Year of death in Jewish gen notes is 1876 not 1872 – leaning towards a transcription error.]

Probate
Ancestry 22nd September 1873
Will of Hyam Levy – Effects under £100

The will of Hyam Levy, late of 36 Middlesex Street, St Botolph, Aldgate in the City of London, Butcher who died 25th November 1872 at Middlesex Street was proved at the Principal Registry by Frances Levy of 36 Middlesex Street widow of the relict the sole executrix.

Frances Napthali

Jewish Name Brynah. Hyam Levy's wife.

Born	1811 Aldgate (Ancestry)
Married	1834 (31st December) (Synagogue scribes)
Died	(Q4) 1888 *(Jewish Chronicle)*
Father	Joseph Naphtali (Synagogue scribes)
Mother	Leah 1781 (Ancestry)
Spouse	Hyam Levy (Synagogue scribes)
Children	Isaac 1836 (Ancestry)

Naphtali 1838 (Ancestry)
Sarah 1840 (Ancestry)
Joseph Hyam 1842 (Ancestry)
Rachael 1843 (JewishGen.org)
Mordecai 1845 (JewishGen.org)
Elias 1848 (Ancestry)
Henry 1850 (Ancestry)
Elizabeth 1855 (Ancestry)
Siblings Morris Naphtali 1806 (1841 census)
Sarah 1810 (1841 census)
Solomon 1815 (1 August) (Synagogue scribes)
Esther 1820 (1841 census)

Timeline

1811 Born (Ancestry)
1811 New Goulston Street (Tax records)
1834 (31st December) Marriage to Frances (Synagogue scribes)
1835 (23rd October) 41½ Petticoat Lane (Insurance policy)
1836 Birth of Isaac (1841 census)
1836 42 Petticoat Lane (*Pigot's Directory*)
1836 (21st April) 41½ Petticoat Lane (Freedom of the City)
1838 Birth of Naphtali (1841 census)
1839 36 Petticoat Lane (*Pigot's Directory*)
1840 36 Middlesex Street (*Pigot's Directory*)
1840 Birth of Sarah (1841 census)
1841 36 Petticoat Lane (1841 census)
1841 Birth of Joseph Hyam (1851 census)
1843 Birth of Rachael (JewishGen.org)
1845 Birth of Mordecai (JewishGen.org)
1846 (18th February) 36 Middlesex Street (Insurance policy)
1848 Birth of Elias (1851 census)
1849 36 Petticoat Lane (1849 *Post Office Directory*)
1850 Birth of Henry (1851 census)
1851 36 Petticoat Lane (1851 census)
1852 6 Middlesex Street (Insurance policy)
1852 (8th July) 36 Middlesex Street (Insurance policy)
1855 Birth of Elizabeth (1861 census)
1861 36 Petticoat Lane (1861 census)

1865 36 Middlesex Street (Post Office Directory, London)
1866 36 Middlesex Street (Post Office Directory, London)

1868 (13th November) 36 Middlesex Street (*Jewish Chronicle* Kosher record)
1871 36 Petticoat Lane (1871 census)
1872 (26th November) Death of Hyam (Ancestry)
1878 36 Middlesex Street (*Jewish Chronicle*)
1880 36 Middlesex Street (*Jewish Chronicle*)
1881 36 Middlesex Street (1881 census)
1888 Died (*Jewish Chronicle*)

Isaac Levy

Hyam Levy's son; Joseph Hyam Levy's brother; Jacob Levy's cousin.

Born   1836 (Ancestry)
Father   Hyam Levy (Ancestry)
Mother   Frances Naphtali (Ancestry)

Timeline

1841 36 Petticoat Lane (1841 census)
1851 36 Petticoat Lane (1851 census)

Notes

JewishGen

Subject ID 25894. Surname Levy, First name Isaac
Born 1836 Aldgate
Father Hyam Levy, Mother Frances Naphtali
Faith Affiliation – Early Great Synagogue Lewin birth rec
1840s Middlesex Street Sibs birthplace
1850s 36 Middlesex Street (1851 census)
1860s 1 Hutchinson Street

While JewishGen does have Isaac living at 1 Hutchinson Street in 1861, we don't agree it's the same person. It would be logical given his brother owned the property and his other brother (Napthali) was living there in the 1871 census, however this Isaac was a glazier, a trade never known in the family and was noted as being born in Russia.

Naphtali Levy

Hyam Levy's son; Joseph Hyam Levy's brother; Jacob Levy's cousin.

Born   1838 (JewishGen.org)
Married   1861 (10th April) (JewishGen.org)
Died   1883 (9th November) (Ancestry)
Father   Hyam Levy (JewishGen.org)
Mother   Frances Naphtali (JewishGen.org)
Spouse   Esther Isaacs (JewishGen.org)
Children   Amelia 1862 (Ancestry)
            Francis 1864 (Ancestry)
            Hyman 1867 (31st January) (Ancestry)
            Leah 1869 (16th January) (Ancestry)
            Elias 1870 (Ancestry)
            Kate 1871 (Ancestry)
            Isaac 1872 (4th December) (Ancestry)
            Joseph 1875 (Ancestry)
            Elizabeth 1878 (Ancestry)

Timeline

1838 Born (JewishGen.org)
1841 36 Petticoat Lane (1841 census)
1851 36 Petticoat Lane (1851 census)
1861 1 Hutchinson Street (1861 census)
1861 (10th April) Marriage to Esther (JewishGen.org)
1862 Birth of Amelia (JewishGen.org)
1864 Birth of Frances (1871 census)
1867 (31st January) Birth of Hyman (Jewish Free Schools)
1869 (16th January) Birth of Leah (1871 census)
1869 118 Middlesex Street (School record)
1870 Birth of Elias (1871 census)
1870 118 Middlesex Street (Electoral Roll)
1871 Birth of Kate (1871 census)
1871 118 Middlesex Street (1871 census)
1872 (May) 118 Middlesex Street (Jewish Free Schools)
1872 (4th December) birth of Isaac (1939 Register)
1873 118 Middlesex Street (Electoral Roll)

1875   118 Middlesex Street & Coach and Horses public house (Electoral Roll)
1875   Birth of Joseph (1881 census)
1876   118 Middlesex Street (Electoral Roll)
1877   118 Middlesex Street (Electoral Roll)
1878   Birth of Kate (1881 census)
1878   118 Middlesex Street (Electoral Roll)
1879   118 Middlesex Street (Electoral Roll)
1880   118 Middlesex Street (Electoral Roll)
1881   111 Mile End Road (1881 census)
1882   111 Mile End Road (Electoral Roll)
1883   111 Mile End Road (Electoral Roll)
1883   (9th November) Death (Newspaper report)
1883   (9th November) 111 Mile End Road (Newspaper report)

Notes

The Jewish Chronicle and Hebrew Observer, 6th August 1858:

PETTICOAT LANE

To the editor of what appeared in the *Daily Telegraph* on Monday last I sent a letter to the editor, of which the following is a copy, but he has not thought proper to insert it.

I remain, sir, yours truly
Naphtali Levy

36 Petticoat Lane Aug. 5th 1858

To the editor of the *Daily Telegraph*.

Sir, I believe it to be the boast of an Englishman that he is impartial and will always hear two sides of a question. I have no doubt this is the case with you. I was rather surprised on reading this day's *Telegraph* (of which I have been a supporter since the commencement) to find a report containing a long account of Petticoat Lane, but as the very same words are in a contemporary paper there must be the same reporter to both, and therefore is not from what you have witnessed yourself you give that account.

Your report says it is a nest of about five hundred wretched houses, built in close courts and alleys, where habitations would be least expected. As regards to that, I beg to say you are misinformed. Instead of being wretched houses, there are no better or cleaner in the Metropolis. Think of the time when cholera raged, only two persons died from it in this neighbourhood.

You then say that very few of these houses are without the means of allowing those that enter one way to leave by another. Of course everybody reading this knows what is meant by it, and as the report all through is calculated to do the inhabitants a great amount of injury, I beg to say that if you or any other gentleman wish to satisfy your minds in that art, every facility will be offered you by the inhabitants, to show that there are hardly any houses with more than one entrance.

You say that there is scarcely a session at the Old Bailey but that the evidence of the police prove that a large portion of the property which is daily stolen is there disposed of. Now there is an old saying "Give a dog an ill name" &c,. Of course the first thing a person will say is that a stolen article must find its way down there. Now we have, I believe, a very clever set of men as detectives, who find such persons as have lately been taken up for railway and bank frauds, and who were also clever at finding the murderer of the woman in the Haymarket. If the Lane were a receptacle for stolen goods, and as the goods are exposed for sale daily, I am sure those gentlemen would not be long finding owners for them, and therefore common sense will tell you that you are wrong. You speak of goods of every description offered for sale, putting it in plain words, "stolen", which is of course what you mean. But if you have ever been in an auction room you will find that most of the buyers are Jews, which will account for the quantity of miscellaneous goods exposed there.

The Lane is almost a necessity to the working classes. Most of the vendors on Sundays are Christians, and depend on that day's earnings to provide bread and meat for their families.

The shopkeepers as a body are as loyal as any in the empire, and we can boast of having no houses of ill fame there, and there are no murders or garotte robberies committed, as in other neighbourhoods.

Hoping you will insert this in justice to the inhabitants, I remain, Sir, yours most respectfully.

Naphtali Levy

Esther Isaacs

Naphtali Levy's wife.

Born	1840 (JewishGen.org)
Married	1861 (10th April) (JewishGen.org)
Died	1917 (Ancestry)
Father	Elias Isaacs (JewishGen.org)
Mother	Amelia Mendoza (JewishGen.org)
Spouse	Naphtali Levy (JewishGen.org)
	Henry Nathan (Ancestry)
Children	Amelia 1862 (Ancestry)
	Francis 1864 (Ancestry)
	Hyman 1867 (31st January) (Ancestry)
	Leah 1869 (16th January) (Ancestry)
	Elias 1870 (Ancestry)
	Kate 1871 (Ancestry)
	Isaac 1872 (4th December) (Ancestry)
	Joseph 1875 (Ancestry)
	Elizabeth 1878 (Ancestry)

Sarah Levy

Hyam Levy's daughter; Joseph Hyam Levy's sister; Jacob Levy's cousin.

Born	1840 (Ancestry)
Father	Hyam Levy (JewishGen.org)
Mother	Frances Naphtali (JewishGen.org)

Timeline

1851	36 Petticoat Lane (1851 census)
1861	36 Petticoat Lane (1861 census)
1871	36 Petticoat Lane (1871 census)
1881	36 Middlesex Street (1881 census)
1891	4 Hutchinson Street (1891 census)
1901	4 Hutchinson Street (1901 census)
1911	4 Hutchinson Street (1911 census)

Notes

Is a lodger at 4 Hutchinson Street in 1911, home of the Saqui family?

Joseph Hyam Levy

The witness. Hyam Levy's son; Jacob Levy's cousin.

Born	(27th June) 1841 (JewishGen.org)
Married	(31st October) 1866 (JewishGen.org)
Died	(16th May) 1914 (*Jewish Chronicle*)
Father	Hyam Levy (JewishGen.org)
Mother	Frances Naphtali (JewishGen.org)
Spouse	Amelia Lewis (JewishGen.org)

Timeline

1841   (27th June) Born (JewishGen.org)
1851   36 Petticoat Lane (1851 census)
1861   36 Petticoat Lane (1861 census)
1866   (31st October) Marriage to Amelia (*Jewish Chronicle*)
1868   1 Hutchinson Street (*Jewish Chronicle*)
1870   1 Hutchinson Street (Electoral Roll)
1871   1 Hutchinson Avenue (1871 census)
1878   1 Hutchinson Street (*Jewish Chronicle*)
1880   (16th January) 1 Hutchinson Street (*Jewish Chronicle*)
1880   (30th January) 1 Hutchinson Street (*Jewish Chronicle*)
1881   1 Hutchinson Street (1881 census)
1885   1 Hutchinson Street (JewishGen.org)
1890   1 Hutchinson Street (Electoral Roll)
1891   1 Hutchinson Street (1891 census)
1891   1 Hutchinson Street (Electoral Roll)
1892   1 Hutchinson Street (Electoral Roll)
1893   1 Hutchinson Street (Electoral Roll)
1898   124 Mildmay Road (Electoral Roll)
1899   124 Mildmay Road (JewishGen.org)
1901   124 Mildmay Road (1901 census)
1905   124 Mildmay Road (Electoral Roll)
1910   124 Mildmay Road (JewishGen.org)
1911   124 Mildmay Road (1911 census)
1912   (4th September) Death of Amelia (*Jewish Chronicle*)

1912   (4th September) 124 Mildmay Road (*Jewish Chronicle*)
1912   (4th September) 124 Mildmay Road (*Jewish Chronicle*)
1914   (16th May) Died (*Jewish Chronicle*)
1914   (16th May) 124 Mildmay Road (*Jewish Chronicle*)

Notes

Jewish Chronicle, 20th September 1912:

On the 4th September 1912 at Brighton, Milly, the beloved wife of Joseph Hyam Levy, 124 Mildmay Road N. May her soul rest in peace.

On the 4th September at Brighton, after a sad and long illness, Amelia, wife of Joseph Hyam Levy and beloved sister of Henry and Moss Lewis, 12 Howitt Road, Belise Park.

Mr J.H.Levy of 124, Mildmay Road returns thanks to his many friends for the marks of sympathy shown during this week of mourning for his late wife.

Jewish Chronicle, 22nd May 1914:

Levy: On the 16th of May at 124 Mildmay Road Canonbury, after a painful illness, Joseph Hyam Levy late of Middlesex Street, dearly beloved brother of Elizabeth Goldberg (nee Betsy Levy). Deeply mourned by his sorrowing sister, nephew and nieces. May his soul rest in peace. Shiva at 16 Steward Street Bishopsgate E.C

Probate

Levy: Joseph Hyam of 124 Mildmay Road, Mildmay Park, Middlesex died 16th May 1914 at West London Hospital, Hammersmith, Middlesex Probate London 9th July to Harry Moss Myers solicitor and Joseph Barnett fruiterer. Effects £2,410 11s 6d.

Jewish Chronicle, 17th July 1914:

Mr Joseph Hyam Levy of 124 Mildmay Road, Mildmay Park who died on May 16th and whose will is proved by Harry Moss of 25 Wormwood Street and Joseph Barnett of 292 Old Ford Road, has left £2,410 11s 6d. He gave his wearing apparel to the Jewish Home of the Incurables: £200 to his sister Elizabeth Goldberg, £100 to Abraham Jacobs; £100 Alfred Levy £100 to Fanny Levy, £50 Ted Levy and the proceeds of the sale of the Hutchinson property to his sister Elizabeth Goldberg after the payment of £100 to Alfred Levy.

The residue of the property is to be divided between St Peter's Hospital, London Hospital, Jewish Hospital, German Hospital, Home and Hospital for the Jewish Incurable, the Home for Aged Jews, Jews Hospital and Orphan Asylum, Victoria Park Hospital, Ophthalmic Hospital City Road Hospital, Aldeman Treloak, Cripples' Home and the Jewish Blind Society.

Jewish Chronicle, 6th November 1914:
Hyam Levy deceased
Joseph Hyam Levy deceased

If Elias Levy, a son of Hyam Levy who died on the 25th day of November 1872 and a brother of Joseph Hyam Levy, late of 124 Mildmay Park N. who died on the 16 day of May 1914 will communicate with Messrs S Myers and Son of 25 Wormwood St London EC he will hear something to his advantage. If the said Elias Levy does not communicate as aforesaid by the 10th day of December 1914 application will be made to the probate court for an order presuming his death. Any person who knows and can give information as to the present address of the said Elias Levy, if living, or if the said Elias Levy is dead can give information as to the date and place of his death, is requested to forthwith communicate with the undersigned.

Dated this 31st day of October 1914.
S.Myers & Son
25 Wormwood St London E.C
Solicitors for the executor of Joseph Hyam Levy

Amelia Levy

Joseph Hyam Levy's wife.

Born	1842 (JewishGen.org)
Married	1866 (31st October) (JewishGen.org)
Died	1912 (4th September) (*Jewish Chronicle*)
Father	Phillip Lewis (JewishGen.org)
Mother	Ann Lyons (JewishGen.org)
Spouse	Joseph Hyam Levy (JewishGen.org)
Siblings	Moses 1839 (Ancestry)
	Henry 1841 (Ancestry)

Timeline

1842   Born (JewishGen.org)

1851   24 Mitre Street (1851 census)
1861   24 Mitre street (1861 census)
1866   (31st October) Marriage to Joseph (*Jewish Chronicle*)
1868   1 Hutchinson Street (*Jewish Chronicle*)
1870   1 Hutchinson Street (Electoral Roll)
1871   1 Hutchinson Avenue (1871 census)
1878   1 Hutchinson Street (*Jewish Chronicle*)
1880   (16th January) 1 Hutchinson Street (*Jewish Chronicle*)
1880   (30th January) 1 Hutchinson Street (*Jewish Chronicle*)
1881   1 Hutchinson Street (1881 census)
1885   1 Hutchinson Street (JewishGen.org)
1890   1 Hutchinson Street (Electoral Roll)
1891   1 Hutchinson Street (1891 census)
1891   1 Hutchinson Street (Electoral Roll)
1892   1 Hutchinson Street (Electoral Roll)
1893   1 Hutchinson Street (Electoral Roll)
1898   124 Mildmay Road (Electoral Roll)
1899   124 Mildmay Road (JewishGen.org)
1901   124 Mildmay Road (1901 census)
1905   124 Mildmay Road (Electoral Roll)
1910   124 Mildmay Road (JewishGen.org)
1911   124 Mildmay Road (1911 census)
1912   (4th September) Died (*Jewish Chronicle*)
1912   (4th September) 124 Mildmay Road (*Jewish Chronicle*)

Notes

Amelia is still at 24 Mitre Street in the 1851 census, but it is now her grandfather's (Henry Lyons) premises. Her parents are a few doors down at 21 Mitre Street. Amelia was niece of Mary Lyons née Barnett, who was sister to the Isaac Barnett who married Elizabeth Levy (Jacob's sister).

Rachael Levy

Hyam Levy's daughter; Joseph Hyam Levy's sister; Jacob Levy's cousin.

Born   1843 (Ancestry)
Father   Hyam Levy (Ancestry)
Mother   Frances Naphtali (Ancestry)

Timeline

1851   36 Petticoat Lane (1851 census)

Notes

Not in the 1851 census: did she die young?

Mordecai Levy

Hyam Levy's son; Joseph Hyam Levy's brother; Jacob Levy's cousin.

Born   1845 (Q1) (JewishGen.org)
Father   Hyam Levy (JewishGen.org)
Mother   Frances Naphtali (JewishGen.org)

Timeline

1851   Born (JewishGen.org)
1851   36 Petticoat Lane (1851 census)

Notes

Not in the 1851 census – did he die young? 'Mordecai' is known to be the Jewish version of the name 'Henry'.

Elias Levy

Hyam Levy's son; Joseph Hyam Levy's brother; Jacob Levy's cousin.

Born   1848 (3rd June) (JewishGen.org)
Married   1870 (Birth, Marriage Death website)
Died   1888-1891 (See Notes)
Father   Hyam Levy (JewishGen.org)
Mother   Frances Naphtali (JewishGen.org)
Spouse   Rachel Jonas (Ancestry)
Children   Hyam 1870 (Ancestry)
             Elias 1873 (Ancestry)
             Frances 1875 (Ancestry)
             Ellen 1876 (Ancestry)
             Alfred 1882 (Ancestry)
             Naphtali 1887 (Ancestry)

Timeline

1848 Born (JewishGen.org)

1851 36 Petticoat Lane (1851 census)

1861 36 Petticoat Lane (1861 census)

1870 Marriage to Rachel (Birth, Marriage Death website)

1870 Birth of Hyam (1871 census)

1871 7 Eastmane Court (1871 census)

1873 Birth of Elias (1881 census)

1875 Birth of Frances (1881 census)

1876 Birth of Ellen (1881 census)

1881 7 Spitalfields (1881 census)

1887 Birth of Naphtali (Ancestry)

1888 (8th May) Admission to Islington Infirmary (Ancestry)

1888 (4th June) Discharge from Infirmary (Ancestry)

1888 1891 Died (See Notes)

Notes

Daughter Frances is noted as being deaf and dumb throughout the census records. While can't find a death registration for Elias in the 1891 census, Rachel is noted as being a widow.

Rachel Jonas
Elias Levy's wife.

Born	1851 (Ancestry)
Married	1870 (Birth, Marriage Death website)
Father	Elias Jonas (Ancestry)
Mother	Ellen Solomons (Ancestry)
Spouse	Elias Levy (Ancestry)
Children	Hyam 1870 (Ancestry)
	Elias 1873 (Ancestry)
	Frances 1875 (Ancestry)
	Ellen 1878 (Ancestry)
	Alfred 1882 (Ancestry)
	Naphtali 1887 (Ancestry)
Siblings	Solomon 1840 (Ancestry)
	Susannah 1841 (Ancestry)
	Michael 1844 (Ancestry)

Jane 1847 (Ancestry)
Samuel 1853 (Ancestry)

Timeline

1851　Born (Birth, Marriage Death website)
1861　12 Palmer Street (1861 census)
1870　Marriage to Elias (Birth, Marriage Death website)
1870　Birth of Hyam (1871 census)
1871　7 Eastmane Court (1871 census)
1873　Birth of Elias (1881 census)
1876　Birth of Francis (1881 census)
1878　Birth of Ellen (1881 census)
1881　7 Spitalfields (1881 census)
1882　Birth of Alfred (1891 census)
1887　Birth of Naphtali (Ancestry)
1887　(19th August)Workhouse entry (Ancestry)
1887　(11th November) Workhouse Discharge (Ancestry)
1888　1901 Death of Elias (See Notes)
1901　25 Tenter Street (1901 census)
1911　30 Elder Street (1911 census)

Henry Levy

Hyam Levy's son; Joseph Hyam Levy's brother; Jacob Levy's cousin.

Born　　　1850 (JewishGen.org)
Father　　Hyam Levy (JewishGen.org)
Mother　　Frances Naphtali (JewishGen.org)

Timeline

1851　36 Petticoat Lane (1851 census)

Notes

Not in the 1861 census, did he die young?

Elizabeth Levy

Hyam Levy's daughter; Joseph Hyam Levy's sister; Jacob Levy's cousin.

Born   1855 (Ancestry)
Married   1892 (Birth, Marriage Death website)
           1904 (June) (Ancestry)
Died   1943 (June) (Ancestry)
Father   Hyam Levy (Ancestry)
Mother   Frances Naphtali (Ancestry)
Spouse   Abraham Jacobs (See Notes)
           Philip Goldberg (Ancestry)
Children   Abraham 1893 (13th February) (Ancestry)

Timeline

1851   36 Petticoat Lane (1851 census)
1861   36 Petticoat Lane (1861 census)
1871   36 Petticoat Lane (1871 census)
1881   36 Middlesex Street (1881 census)
1891   4 Hutchinson Street (1891 census)
1892   Married to Abraham Jacobs (See Notes)
1893   (13th February) Birth of Abraham (School records)
1901   4 Hutchinson Avenue (1901 census)
1904   (June) married Philip Goldberg (Ancestry)

Notes

JewishGen Hopital database

Abraham Jacobs, Jews Hospital
Date of birth 13th February 1893, 4 Hutchinson Avenue, Houndsditch

Ancestry School records

City of London Gravel Lane School
Name Abraham Jacobs
Date of admission 22/06/96
No. 93
Parent Elizabeth, Needlewoman, 4 Hutchinson Street
Date of birth 13/02/93
Transferred to B dept

Grayhurst Road School

Name Jacobs, Abram
Admitted 15/10/1906
No. 2055
Parent Phillip
Date of birth 13/02/93, 112 Brougham Road

* * *

JACOB LEVY'S FAMILY

Jacob Levy
The suspect; Jewish name Joseph. Joseph Hyam Levy's cousin.

Born   1856 (11th March) (Birth certificate)
Married   1879 (23rd April) (Marriage certificate)
Died   1891 (29th July) (Death certificate)
Father   Joseph Levy (Birth certificate)
Mother   Caroline Levy (Birth certificate)
Spouse   Sarah Abrahams (Marriage certificate)
Children   Joseph 1879 (17th August) (Ancestry)
           Isaac 1881 (15th January) (Ancestry)
           Lewis 1883 (20th January) (Ancestry)
           Hannah 1885 (Ancestry)
           Nathan 1886 (8th June) (Birth certificate)
           John/Jacob 1887 (14th October) (Birth certificate)
           Caroline 1889 (Q1) (Ancestry)
           Moss 1890 (18th July) (Ancestry)

Timeline

1856   (11th March) Born (Birth certificate)
1856   (11th March) 111 Middlesex Street (Birth certificate)
1861   111 Middlesex Street (1861 census)
1871   111 Middlesex Street (1871 census)
1875   (19th May) Death of Abraham (Newspaper article)
1875   (19th May) 111 Middlesex Street (Newspaper article)
1878   11 Fieldgate Street (*Jewish Chronicle*)
1879   (23rd April) Marriage to Sarah Abrahams (Marriage certificate)

1879   (23rd April) 111 Middlesex Street (Marriage certificate)
1879   (17th August) Birth of Joseph (1939 Register)
1880   11 Fieldgate Street (*Jewish Chronicle*)
1881   (15th January) Birth of Isaac (1939 Register)
1881   11 Fieldgate Street (1881 census)
1883   (20th January) Birth of Lewis (1939 Register)
1885   Birth of Hannah (1891 census)
1886   (10th March) arrested (Old Bailey records)
1886   36 Middlesex Street (Old Bailey records)
1886   (19th March) Death of father (Death certificate)
1886   (5th April) found guilty of theft (Asylum records)
1886   (5th April) sent to Holloway (Asylum records)
1886   (19th April) sent to Chelmsford Prison (Asylum records)
1886   (21st May) sent to Essex Insane Asylum (Asylum records)
1886   (8th June) Birth of Nathan (Birth certificate)
1887   (3rd February) Release from asylum (Asylum records)
1887   (14th October) Birth of Jacob (Birth certificate)
1887   (14th October) 36 Middlesex Street (Birth certificate)
1888   36 Middlesex Street (*Business Traders Directory*)
1890   (Q1) Birth of Caroline (Birth, Marriage Death website)
1890   (14th August) admitted to Stone asylum (Asylum records)
1890   (14th August) 36 Middlesex Street (Asylum records)
1890   (18th July) Birth of Moss (1939 Register)
1891   Stone House Hospital (1891 census)
1891   (29th July) Died (Death certificate)
1891   (29th July) Stone House Hospital (Death certificate)

Sarah Abrahams
Jacob Levy's wife.

Born	1857 (Ancestry)
Married	1879 (23rd April) (Marriage certificate)
Died	1925 (3rd February) (*Jewish Chronicle*)
Father	Isaac Abrahams (Marriage certificate)
Mother	Phoebe Levy (Marriage certificate)
Spouse	Jacob Levy (Marriage certificate)
Children	Joseph 1879 (17th August) (Ancestry)
	Isaac 1881 (15th April) (Ancestry)

Lewis 1883 (20th January) (Ancestry)
Hannah 1885 (1891 census)
Nathan 1886 (8th June) (Birth certificate)
John/Jacob 1887 (14th October) (Birth certificate)
Caroline 1889 (Q1) (Birth, Marriage Death website)
Moss 1890 (18 July) (Ancestry)

Siblings   Nathan 1858 (Ancestry)
Rachael 1862 (Ancestry)
Myer 1864 (29th September) (JewishGen.org)
Flora [Harris] 1867 (Ancestry)
Abraham 1868 (9th July) (Ancestry)
Michael (Mike) 1871 (Ancestry)
Mark 1973 (Ancestry)
Rebecca [Erlich] 1875 (12th February) (Ancestry)
Phillip 1877 (Ancestry)
Esther [Marks] 1879 (Ancestry)

Timeline

1857   Born (1871 census)
1871   4 Bull Court (1871 census)
1879   (23rd April) Marriage to Jacob (Marriage certificate)
1879   (23rd April) 111 Middlesex Street (Marriage certificate)
1879   (17th August) Birth of Joseph (1939 Register)
1880   11 Fieldgate Street *(Jewish Chronicle)*
1881   (15th January) Birth of Isaac (1939 Register)
1881   11 Fieldgate Street (1881 census)
1883   (20th January) Birth of Lewis (1939 Register)
1885   Birth of Hannah (1891 census)
1886   (10th March) Jacob arrested (Old Bailey records)
1886   36 Middlesex Street (Old Bailey records)
1886   (5th April) found guilty of theft (Asylum records)
1886   (5th April) sent to Holloway (Asylum records)
1886   (19th April) sent to Chelmsford Prison (Asylum records)
1886   (21st May) sent to Essex Insane Asylum (Asylum records)
1886   (8th June) Birth of Nathan (Birth certificate)
1886   (8th June) 36 Middlesex Street (Birth certificate)
1887   (3rd February) Jacob released from asylum (Asylum records)
1887   (14th October) Birth of Jacob (Birth certificate)

1887 (14th October) 36 Middlesex Street (Birth certificate)
1888 36 Middlesex Street (Business Traders Directory)
1890 (Q1) Birth of Caroline (Birth, Marriage Death website)
1890 (14th August) Jacob admitted to Stone asylum (Asylum records)
1890 (14th August) 36 Middlesex Street (Asylum records)
1890 (18th July) Birth of Moss (1939 Register)
1891 (February) Death of Emma Holyoake (Newspaper report)
1891 (February) 69 Middlesex Street (Newspaper report)
1891 69 Middlesex Street (1891 census)
1891 (29th July) Jacob died (Death certificate)
1901 7 New Street (1901 census)
1904 (24th March) Death of Caroline (Death certificate)
1904 7 New Street (Death certificate)
1911 8 Graces Alley (1911 census)
1925 (3rd February) Died (*Jewish Chronicle*)

Notes

Burial, East Ham: Sarah Levy 5/02/1925 – C-20-22.

Sarah never actually moved, even though her address changed from 36 Middlesex Street to 69 Middlesex Street; there was just a renumbering at the end of the 1880s.

The 1911 census intake showed Sarah living at 7 Graces Alley with her sons Nathan, John and Moss. Nathan Freshwater, living next door is his brother Abraham Freshwater and his wife Hannah née Levy. On the next sheet, but also at 8 Graces Alley, is Sarah Levy (Hannah's mother) with Nathan, John and Moss.Next door at 14 Graces Alley were Phillip and Rosetta Solomons. On the next sheet, but also at 14 Graces Alley, were Lewis Levy and Dinah née Solomons.

Reynolds's Newspaper, 22nd February 1891:

STRANGE SUICIDE OF A SERVANT

Wynne E. Baxter, coroner for East End of London, held an inquest on Thursday at the London Hospital respecting the death of Emma Holyoake, aged twenty four, a domestic servant, late in service at 69 Middlesex Street. EC.

Emma Holyoake, the wife of a boot finisher of 68, Treadway Street, Bethnal

Green, deposed that the deceased was her husband's cousin. On Monday she saw the deceased in the hospital. The deceased said, "My missus made me do it. She said you would turn me out when I came home." The deceased had appeared strange at times, and some of her relatives had been in lunatic asylums.

Sarah Levy, the wife of a butcher, deposed that the deceased had been in her service for two and a half years. Between half past three and four p.m. on Monday witness's sister went upstairs, and then came down and said that the deceased was lying in a pool of blood. Assistance was obtained, and the deceased was removed to the hospital. The deceased had quarrelled with the witness's brother because he blacked her face at Christmas. She gave witness notice of her intention to leave, as she wanted to be a "washer-up at the Tee-to-Tum".

Sergeant Young, City Police deposed that he found the deceased lying on her back in the back room on the third floor, with her throat cut, and a number of wounds about the chest. Both in the back and front rooms there were pools of blood. The small butcher's knife produced was found lying by her side.

Dr Snook, house surgeon, deposed that the deceased was suffering from two large jagged wounds in the neck, one of which had cut the windpipe. There were also two stabs on the neck, six severe cuts on the left side of the chest and eight punctured wounds.

The jury after a lengthy inquiry returned a verdict of 'Suicide whilst temporarily insane.'

Joseph Levy

Jacob Levy's son.

Born	1879 (17th August) (See Notes)
Married	1904 (Q1) (Ancestry)
Died	1953 (Q1) (Ancestry)
Father	Jacob Levy (Ancestry)
Mother	Sarah Abrahams (Ancestry)
Spouse	Lillian/Leah Driver (Ancestry)
Children	Caroline Levy (Q1) (Birth, Marriage Death website)

Timeline

1879   (17th August) Born (1939 Register)
1881   11 Fieldgate Street (1881 census)
1891   69 Middlesex Street (1891 census)
1901   7 New Street (1901 census)
1901   (29th July) Death of Jacob (Asylum Record)
1908   (Q1) Birth of Caroline (Birth, Marriage Death website)
1911   77 Vallance Road (1911 census)
1925   (3rd February) Death of Sarah (*Jewish Chronicle*)
1925   (3rd February) 3 Gloucester Place (*Jewish Chronicle*)
1939   8 Western Place (1939 Register)
1953   (Q1) Died (See Notes)

Notes

Possible for Joseph and Lily in 1939 under the name Driver. We have them in Brighton in 1925. In the 1939 Register they were living at 8 Western Road, Brighton. The date of birth for Lily is identical to that of Lily Driver who married Joseph Levy. Also, Driver was Lily's maiden name. If this is them, then the deaths were in the name of Driver.

In addition, there was no Joseph Levy born within the whole of 1879 (BMD register), but there was a Joseph Levy born in the same quarter of 1879.

There were two children noted in the 1911 census, both living, but we can only find Caroline details.

Lily Driver

Joseph Levy's wife.

Born   1881 (30th June) (Ancestry)
Married   1904 (Q1) (Ancestry)
Died   1953 (Q4) (See Notes)
Father   Morris Driver (Ancestry)
Mother   Caroline Springer (Ancestry)
Spouse   Joseph Levy (Ancestry)
Children   Caroline Levy 1981 (Q1) (Birth, Marriage Death
website)

Timeline

1881   (30th June) Born (1939 Register)

1901 77 Vallance Road (1901 census)
1908 (Q1) Birth of Caroline (Birth, Marriage Death website)
1911 77 Vallance Road (1911 census)
1925 3 Gloucester Place *(Jewish Chronicle)*
1939 8 Western Road (1939 census)
1953 (Q4) Died (See Notes)

Notes

Possible for Joseph and Lily in 1939 under the name Driver. We have them in Brighton in 1925. In the 1939 Register they were living at 8 Western Road Brighton. The date of birth for Lily is identical to that of Lily Driver who married Joseph Levy. Also Driver was Lily's maiden name. If this is them then the deaths were in the name of Driver.

In addition, there was no Joseph Levy born within the whole of 1879 (BMD register), but there was a Joseph Levy born in the same quarter of 1879.

Throughout the records the name changes between Lily and Leah, but research shows that 'Leah' is a Hebrew name of 'Lily' so we're assuming these are the same person.

Jewish Chronicle, Friday 17th September 1926:

The engagement between Mr Louis Harris of 18 Sillwood Road Brighton and Miss Carrie Levy (Driver) of 3 Gloucester Place, Brighton is now cancelled.

Isaac Levy

Jacob Levy's son.

Born	1881 (15th January) (Ancestry)
Married	1907 (15th April) (JewishGen.org)
Died	1956 (11th July) (Ancestry)
Spouse	Hannah Harris (JewishGen.org)
Father	Jacob Levy (JewishGen.org)
Mother	Sarah Abrahams (Ancestry)
Children	Sarah [Cross] 1907 (21st June) (Ancestry)
	Phoebe 1910 (Ancestry)
	Lily [Bilkin] 1911 (20th June) (Ancestry)
	Rebecca [Shulman] 1913 (Ancestry)
	Caroline 1916 (28th February) (Ancestry)

Jennie [Leander] 1918 (8th December) (Ancestry)
Elizabeth [Gilard] 1920 (Ancestry)

Timeline

1881 (15th January) Born (1939 Register)
1881 11 Fieldgate Street (1881 census)
1891 69 Middlesex Street (1891 census)
1901 7 New Street (1901 census)
1901 (29th July) Death of Jacob (Asylum Record)
1907 (15th April) Marriage to Hannah Harris (JewishGen.org)
1907 (15th April) 3 Sandys Row (JewishGen.org)
1907 (21st June) Birth of Sarah (1939 Register)
1910 Birth of Phoebe (1911 census)
1911 1 Rosetta Place Sandys Row (1911 census)
1911 (20th June) Birth of Lily (1939 Register)
1913 Birth of Rebecca (Ancestry)
1916 (28th February) Birth of Caroline (1939 Register)
1918 (8th December) Birth of Jennie (1939 Register)
1920 Birth of Elizabet (Ancestry)
1925 (3rd February) Death of Sarah *(Jewish Chronicle)*
1925 (3rd February) 1 Broussin Place *(Jewish Chronicle)*
1939 123 Middlesex Street (1939 Register)
1956 123 Middlesex Street (Probate)

Notes

Jewish Gen marriage records: Sandys Row book 3 no 59
Isaac Levy, 26, Cabinet Maker (Journeyman)
        3 Sandys Row, 15 April 1907, Father Jacob Levy, Butcher
Hannah Harris, 23
        1a Sandys Row, 15 April 1907, Father Mark Harris, Cigarmaker

Probate records
Isaac Levy of 123 Middlesex Street, Bishopsgate, London E1 died 11 July
1956. Administration: London, 10 September to Hannah Levy widow.
Effects £143 16s 9d

Hannah Harris

Isaac Levy's wife.

Born   1883 (23rd July) (Ancestry)
Married   1907 (15th April) (JewishGen.org)
Died   (23th June) 1972 *(Jewish Chronicle)*
Father   Mark Harris (JewishGen.org)
Mother   Phoebe (Ancestry)
Spouse   Isaac Levy (JewishGen.org)
Children   Sarah [Cross] 1907 (21st June) (Ancestry)
            Phoebe [Graham] 1910 (Ancestry)
            Lily [Belkin] 1911 (20th June) (Ancestry)
            Caroline 1916 (28th February) (Ancestry)
            Jennie 1918 (8th December) (Ancestry)
            Rebecca [Shulman] 1913 (Ancestry)
            Elizabeth [Gilard] 1920 (Ancestry)
Siblings   Rebecca 1879 (Ancestry)
            David 1882 (Ancestry)
            Michael 1888 (Ancestry)
            Jane 1893 (Ancestry)
            Clara [Winter] 1895 (Ancestry)
            Alfred 1898 (Ancestry)

Timeline

1883   (23rd July) Born (1939 Register)
1891   1 Sandys Row (1891 census)
1901   1 Sandys Row (1901 census)
1907   (15th April) Marriage to Isaac Levy (JewishGen.org; Marriage record)
1907   (15th April) 3 Sandys Row (JewishGen.org; Marriage record)
1907   (21st June) Birth of Sarah (1939 Register)
1910   Birth of Phoebe (1911 census)
1911   1 Rosetta Place Sandys Row (1911 census)
1911   (20th June) Birth of Lily (1939 Register)
1913   Birth of Rebecca (Ancestry)
1916   (28th February) Birth of Caroline (1939 Register)
1918   (8th December) Birth of Jennie (1939 Register)
1920   Birth of Elizabeth (Ancestry)

1939   123 Middlesex Street (1939 Register)
1956   (11th July) Death of Isaac (Ancestry; Probate)
1956   (11th July) 123 Middlesex Street (Ancestry; Probate)
1972   (23rd June) Died (*Jewish Chronicle*)

Lewis Levy
Jacob Levy's son.

Born   1883 (30th June) (Ancestry)
Married   1905 (29th October) (JewishGen.org)
Father   Jacob Levy (JewishGen.org)
Mother   Sarah Abrahams (Ancestry)
Wife   Dinah Solomons (JewishGen.org)
Children   Jack 1906 (Ancestry)
Phillip1908 (Ancestry)
              Rosetta Nancy [Candler] 1911 (14th June) (Ancestry)
              Sarah 1916 (15th April) (Ancestry)
              Hannah [Bentley] 1919 (31st May) (Ancestry)

Timeline
1883   (30th June) Born (1939 Register)
1891   69 Middlesex Street (1891 census)
1891   (29 July) Death of Father (Asylum records)
1901   7 New Street (1901 census)
1905   (29th October) Marriage to Dinah Solomons (JewishGen.org)
1906   Birth of Jack (1911 census)
1908   Birth of Phillip (1911 census)
1911   14 Graces Alley (1911 census)
1911   (14th June) Birth of Rosetta (1939 Register)
1916   (15th April) Birth of Sarah (1939 Register)
1919   (31st May) Birth of Hannah (1939 Register)
1925   (3rd February) Death of mother (JewishGen.org article)
1925   8 Graces Alley (JewishGen.org) article
1939   7 White Street (1939 Register)
1955   (29th October) Golden wedding (*Jewish Chronicle*)

Notes

Jewishgen marriage records: Sandys Row Book 3 No10
Lewis Levy, 22, Cigar Maker, 6 Graces Alley, 29 Oct 1905
Father – Jacob Levy, Butcher
Dinah Solomons, 18, 17 Graces Alley, 29 Oct 1905
Father – Philip Solomons, Fishmonger

Jewish Chronicle, 28th October 1955
Mr and Mrs Levy (Dinah Solomons) happily announce their Golden
wedding anniversary, October 29th 1955.

Dinah Solomons

Lewis Levy's wife.

Born	1886 (27th December) (Ancestry)
Married	1905 (29th October) (JewishGen.org)
Father	Phillip Solomons (JewishGen.org)
Mother	Rosetta Nathan (Ancestry)
Spouse	Isaac Levy (JewishGen.org)
Children	Jack 1906 (Ancestry)
	Phillip 1908 (Ancestry)
	Rosetta Nancy [Candler] 1911 (14th June) (Ancestry)
	Sarah 1916 (15th April) (Ancestry)
	Hannah [Bentley] 1919 (31st May) (Ancestry)

Timeline

1886 (27th December) Born (1939 Register)
1891 16 Graces Alley (1891 census)
1891 (17th September) 16 Graces Alley (School record)
1894 (26th February) 133 Leman Street (School record)
1901 7 Graces Alley (1901 census)
1905 (29th October) Marriage to Isaac Levy (JewishGen.org)
1906 Birth of Jack (1911 census)
1908 Birth of Phillip (1911 census)
1911 14 Graces Alley (1911 census)
1911 (14th June) Birth of Rosetta (1939 Register)
1916 (15th April) Birth of Sarah (1939 Register)
1919 (31st May) Birth of Hannah (1939 Register)

1925   8 Graces Alley (JewishGen.org)
1939   7 White Street (1939 Register)
1955   (29th October) Golden wedding (*Jewish Chronicle*)

Notes

According to the 1911 census Dinah had one sibling, but no longer living. We have been unable to locate.

School records

Tower Hamlets Betts School
Name Dinah Solomons
Date of birth 26th December 1886
Admission No. 2258
Date of admission 17th September 1891
Father Phillip
Address 16 Graces Alley

Tower Hamlets Berner Street
Name Dinah Solomons
Date of birth 26th December 1886
Admission No. 1755
Date of admission 26th February 1894
Father Phillip, fishmonger
Address 133 Leman Street

By 1917 Dinah's mother Rosetta had moved from 14 Graces Alley to 8 Graces Alley, her address at the time of her death in 1917.

Hannah Levy

Jacob Levy's daughter.

Born	1885 (Ancestry)
Married	1907 (Q3) (Birth, Marriage Death website)
Died	1940 (Ancestry)
Father	Jacob Levy (Ancestry)
Mother	Sarah Abrahams (Ancestry)
Spouse	Abraham Freshwater (Ancestry)
Children	Lewis 1908 (6th June) (Ancestry)
Joseph	1911 (16th February) (Ancestry)

Timeline

1885 Born (Ancestry)
1891 69 Middlesex Street (1891 census)
1891 (29th July) Death of Jacob (Asylum Records)
1901 7 Graces Alley (1901 census)
1907 (Q3) Marriage to Abraham Freshwater (Birth, Marriage Death)
1908 (6th June) Birth of Lewis (1939 Register)
1911 (16th February) Birth of Joseph (1939 Register)
1911 8 Graces Alley (1911 census)
1917 9 Graces Alley (Enlistment papers)
1919 25 Wellclose Square (Discharge papers)
1919 25 Wellclose Square (Electoral Roll)
1925 (3rd February) Death of Sarah (*Jewish Chronicle*)
1925 (3rd February) 48 Streatley Buildings (*Jewish Chronicle*)
1927 48 Streatley Buildings (Electoral Roll)
1930 48 Streatley Buildings (Electoral Roll)
1932 48 Strealety Buildings (Electoral Roll)
1934 48 Streatley Buildings (Electoral Roll)
1937 48 Streatley Buildings (Electoral Roll)
1939 48 Streatley Buildings (Electoral Roll)
1940 Died (Ancestry)

Notes

While Hannah wasn't listed in the 1939 Register with her family, Abraham was classed as married and not a widower. There is a Hannah Freshwater in the 1939 Register, a blind refugee, that could be her. However as we don't have enough information to be sure we haven't put her down as a certain.

Abraham Freshwater

Hannah Levy's husband.

Born	1882 (11th December) (Ancestry)
Married	1907 (Q3) (Birth, Marriage Death website)
Died	1964 (Birth, Marriage Death website)
Father	Levy Freshwater (Ancestry)
Mother	Esther (Ancestry)
Spouse	Hannah Levy (Ancestry)
Children	Lewis 1908 (6th June) (Ancestry)

	Joseph 1911 (16th February) (Ancestry)
Siblings	Phoebe 1868 (Ancestry)
	Michael 1869 (Ancestry)
	Aaron 1871 (Ancestry)
	Samuel 1873 (Ancestry)
	Benjamin 1876 (Ancestry)
	Hane 1878 (Ancestry)
	Nathan 1880 (Ancestry)

Timeline

1882 (11th December) Born (1939 Register)
1891 6 Ringers Buildings (1891 census)
1901 3 Essex Street (1901 census)
1907 (Q3) Marriage to Hannah Levy (Birth, Marriage Death website)
1908 (6th June) Birth of Lewis (1939 Register)
1911 (16th February) Birth of Joseph (1939 Register)
1911 8 Graces Alley (1911 census)
1917 9 Graces Alley (Enlistment papers)
1919 25 Wellclose Square (Discharge papers)
1919 25 Wellclose Square (Electoral Roll)
1925 48 Streatley Buildings (*Jewish Chronicle*)
1927 48 Streatley Buildings (Electoral Roll)
1930 48 Streatley Buildings (Electoral Roll)
1932 48 Strealety Buildings (Electoral Roll)
1934 48 Streatley Buildings (Electoral Roll)
1937 48 Streatley Buildings (Electoral Roll)
1939 48 Streatley Buildings (Electoral Roll)
1939 48 Streatley Buildings (1939 Register)
1940 Death of Hannah (Ancestry)
1964 Died (Birth, Marriage Death website)

Notes

Granted the Victorian and British War medals for services to his country from 1914-19.

Nathan Levy

Jacob Levy's son.

Born	1886 (8th June) (Birth certificate)
Father	Jacob Levy (Birth certificate)
Mother	Sarah Abrahams (Birth certificate)

Timeline

1886 (8th June) Born (Birth certificate)
1886 (8th June) 36 Middlesex Street (Birth certificate)
1891 69 Middlesex Street (1891 census)
1891 (29th July) Death of Jacob (Asylum Record)
1901 7 New Street (1901 census)
1911 7 Graces Alley (1911 census)
1925 (3rd February) Death of Sarah (JewishGen.org)
1925 11½ Cable Street London Docks (*Jewish Chronicle*)

John/Jacob Levy

Jacob Levy's son.

Born	1887 (14th October) (Birth certificate)
Father	Jacob Levy (Birth certificate)
Mother	Sarah Abrahams (Birth certificate)

Timeline

1887 (14th October) Born (Birth certificate)
1887 (14th October) 36 Middlesex Street (Birth certificate)
1891 69 Middlesex Street (1891 census)
1901 7 New Street (1901 census)
1901 (29th July) Death of Jacob (Asylum Record)
1911 8 Graces Alley (1911 census)
1925 (3rd February) Death of Sarah *(Jewish Chronicle)*
1925 8 River Street Clerkenwell *(Jewish Chronicle)*

Caroline Levy

Jacob Levy's daughter.

Born	1889 (Q1) (Birth, Marriage Death website)
Died	1904 (24 March) (Death certificate)

Father   Jacob Levy (Death certificate)
Mother   Sarah Abrahams (1891 census)

Timeline

1889   (Q1) Born (Birth, Marriage Death website)
1891   69 Middlesex Street (1891 census)
1891   (29th July) Death of Jacob (Asylum Record)
1901   1 Ely Terrace (1901 census)
1904   (24th March) Died (Death certificate)
1904   (24th March) 7 New Street (Death certificate)

Notes

Caroline was with her grandparents (Sarah's parents) in the 1901 census. Caroline was 14 year old when she died of acute tuberculosis and tuberculosis. Her brother Isaac was the informant of her death.

Moss Levy

Jacob Levy's son.

Born   1890 (18th July) (Ancestry)
Married   1919 (Q3) (Birth, Marriage Death website)
Father   Jacob Levy (Ancestry)
Mother   Sarah Abrahams (Ancestry)
Spouse   Fanny Metselaar (Ancestry)
Death   1966 (13th June) (Ancestry)

Timeline

1890   (18th July) Born (Ancestry)
1891   69 Middlesex Street (1891 census)
1891   (29th July) Death of Jacob (Asylum Record)
1901   7 New Street (1901 census)
1911   8 Graces Alley (1911 census)
1919   (Q3) Marriage to Fanny Metselaar (Birth, Marriage Deaths)
1925   (3rd February) Death of Sarah (JewishGen.org)
1925   (3rd February) 97 E Block Stepney Green Dwellings (JewishGen.org)
1931   97 Stepney Green Dwellings (Polling Sheet)
1939   39 Stepney Green Dwellings (1939 Register)
1966   (13th June) Died (Probate)

1966   (13th June) 39 Stepney Green Dwellings Probate

Notes

Probate: Moss Lev of 39 Stepney Green Dwellings, Stepney Green E1 died 13th June 1966 at London Hospital, London E1. Administration London, 26th August to Fanny Levy widow £688. [This is an educated guess on our part and may not be the correct Moss. Given the info though, we strongly lean towards it].

Fanny Metselaar

Moss Levy's wife.

Born	1896 (9th October) (Ancestry)
Married	1919 (Q3) (Birth, Marriage Death website)
Father	Alexander Metselaar (Ancestry)
Mother	Eva Pezaro (Ancestry)
Spouse	Moss Levy (Ancestry)
Death	1975 (27th April) (Ancestry)

Timeline

1886   (9th October) Born (Ancestry)
1891   46 Wentworth Street (1891 census)
1911   10 Alexandra Buildings (1911 census)
1919   (Q3) Marriage to Moss Levy (Birth, Marriage Death website)
1925   (3rd February) 97 E Block Stepney Green Dwellings (JewishGen.org)
1931   97 Stepney Green Dwellings (Polling Sheet)
1939   39 Stepney Green Dwellings (1939 Register)
1966   (13th June) Died (Probate)
1966   (13th June) 39 Stepney Green Dwellings (Probate)

ACKNOWLEDGEMENTS

A wealth of love and gratitude to my family and friends for all the years of endless research talks, missed get-togethers and annoying phone calls at all hours; also for not strangling me in my sleep.

A special thank you to my co-author and dad Neil, for never once doubting me in life and for showing me you can never give up on your dreams regardless of what life throws at you.

To my partner Nige, who basically looked after me while I lost myself in endless hours of research, and at times dragged me out for some actual fresh air.

To my mam: you always gave me the strength and determination to overcome the challenges life throws at us.

To my sister Donna, aunty Chris, son Nathan, and nephew Thomas: you all inspire me everyday.

Huge thanks to my friend, fellow researcher and publisher Adam Wood, who has supported us from before we even had the idea of turning our research into a book. Without him this book would never have been written.

Special thanks to some amazing researchers I get to also call friends:

Rob Clack: Thank you for your help and advice over the past few years. Your unwavering belief in me, for not getting sick of my neverending conversations and for your help with the book. and for always telling me how it is – good or bad.

Chris Phillips: I will be forever indebted to you for your patience with my endless questions, and how you patiently helped teach me how to research. I would also love to acknowledge your generosity and contribution of material without question.

Debra Arif: A huge thank you for all your support, and again your generosity in sharing information with us when you could have used it yourself.

Adam Went: What can I say? The years of conversations and putting the world to rights have given me some great memories.

Karen Sweet: Thank you for always checking up on me and for all your support, not just in the book but in my life as a whole.

Further thanks to David Hall, Amanda Lloyd, Martin Harvey, Steve Blomer, Marie McKay, Tom Wescott, Paul Begg, Andrew Firth, Robert Anderson, How and Nina Brown, Jon Horlor, Karsten Giese, Neil Storey, Nemo, Justin Dombrowski, Mark Ripper and John Malcolm,

Also thanks you to a few special people who are no longer with us. Katherine Amin, an inspirational lady; not just in Ripperology but in life in general. Suzi Hanney, a lovely, lovely lady who always had a smile and a joke for people and is still much missed. Chris Scott, An amazing researcher who would always take the time to help you. All are greatly missed by many of us.

TRACY I'ANSON
July 2020

BIBLIOGRAPHY

Jewishgen, which included Insurance records and Business listings
1851 Anglo-jewry database
UK Birth, Marriage and Death records
Jews Free School Spitalfields
London Jews (pre-1850)
Jewish surnames in London Registers Insurance policies
Islington Jews database
Synagogue scribes
Cemetery scribes
United Synagogues
Ancestry
FindMyPast
The Jewish Victorian: Doreen Berger 1861-1870 and 1871-1880
The Great Synagogue Marriage Register 1791-1850
National Archives
Old Bailey online
Free BMD
Casebook.org
JTRForums.com
Ripperologist magazine

JACOB THE RIPPER

Stewart P Evans & Keith Skinner, *The Jack the Ripper Sourcebook*
Paul Begg, *Jack the Ripper: The Facts*

INDEX

211

INDEX

CPSIA information can be obtained
at www.ICGtesting.com
Printed in the USA
JSHW041637290421
14127JS00001B/9